W9-BKE-131

FIFTY MORE PLACES TO PLAY GOLF

BEFORE YOU DIE

FIFTY MORE PLACES TO
PLAY GOLF
BEFORE YOU DIE

**Golf Experts Share the
World's Greatest Destinations**

Chris Santella

FOREWORD BY JEFF WALLACH

STEWART, TABORI & CHANG

NEW YORK

This little book is for Deidre, Cassidy Rose, and Annabel Blossom, and for everyone who enjoys the thrill of stepping onto the first tee of a course they've never played.

✳

Fifty Places to Dive Before You Die:
Diving Experts Share the World's Greatest Destinations

Fifty Places to Fly Fish Before You Die:
Fly-Fishing Experts Share the World's Greatest Destinations

Fifty Places to Go Birding Before You Die:
Birding Experts Share the World's Greatest Destinations

Fifty Places to Play Golf Before You Die:
Golf Experts Share the World's Greatest Destinations

Fifty Places to Sail Before You Die:
Sailing Experts Share the World's Greatest Destinations

Fifty Favorite Fly-Fishing Tales:
Expert Anglers Share Stories from the Sea and Stream

Contents

Acknowledgments 8 / Foreword 9 / Introduction 11

THE DESTINATIONS

(1) **Alberta:** Jasper Park Golf Club 17
RECOMMENDED BY BOB WEEKS

(2) **Arizona:** Talking Stick (South Course) 20
RECOMMENDED BY TIM GREENWELL

(3) **Australia–Perth:** Golf Club at Kennedy Bay 24
RECOMMENDED BY SPENCER SCHAUB

(4) **Australia–Tasmania:** Barnbougle Dunes 27
RECOMMENDED BY MICHAEL CLAYTON

(5) **British Columbia:** Capilano Golf and Country Club 31
RECOMMENDED BY DOUG ROXBURGH

(6) **California–Moorpark:** Rustic Canyon Golf Course 35
RECOMMENDED BY GEOFF SHACKELFORD

(7) **California–Pebble Beach:** Cypress Point Club 39
RECOMMENDED BY JOE PASSOV

(8) **California–San Francisco:** Harding Park 43
RECOMMENDED BY FRANK D. "SANDY" TATUM JR.

(9) **China–Kunming:** Spring City Golf and Lake Resort 48
RECOMMENDED BY GORDON DALGLEISH

(10) **China–Lijiang:** Jade Dragon Snow Mountain Golf Club 51
RECOMMENDED BY JEFF WALLACH

(11) **England–Southport:** Merseyside 57
RECOMMENDED BY BOB WOOD

(12) **England–Westward Ho!:** Royal North Devon 60
RECOMMENDED BY RAN MORRISSETT

(13) **France–Corsica:** Sperone Golf Club 63
RECOMMENDED BY CHRISTOPHER SMITH

(14) **France–Greater Paris:** Chantilly and Fontainebleau 67
RECOMMENDED BY JAMES DODSON

15   **Hawaii–Big Island:** Mauna Kea 73
RECOMMENDED BY DARRIN GEE

16   **Hawaii–Kauai:** Princeville 77
RECOMMENDED BY AMY ALCOTT

17   **Hungary:** Driving the Danube 81
RECOMMENDED BY JIM LAMONT

18   **Illinois:** The Glen Club 87
RECOMMENDED BY JOSH LESNIK

19   **Indonesia:** Nirwana Bali Golf Course 91
RECOMMENDED BY BOB HARRISON

20   **Ireland–Enniscrone:** Enniscrone Golf Club 94
RECOMMENDED BY JOHN STEINBACH

21   **Ireland–Kinsale:** Old Head Golf Links 99
RECOMMENDED BY KEITH BAXTER

22   **Italy:** Bogogno Golf Club 103
RECOMMENDED BY ROBERT VON HAGGE

23   **Jamaica:** White Witch 106
RECOMMENDED BY RICK BARIL

24   **Japan:** Hirono Golf Club 109
RECOMMENDED BY BEN COWAN-DEWAR

25   **Maryland:** Congressional Country Club (Blue Course) 113
RECOMMENDED BY ROBERT MORRIS

26   **Massachusetts:** Farm Neck Golf Club 118
RECOMMENDED BY DAVID BAUM

27   **Mexico–Jalisco:** El Tamarindo 121
RECOMMENDED BY EVAN SCHILLER

28   **Mexico–Playa del Carmen:** El Camaleón at Mayakoba 125
RECOMMENDED BY FRED FUNK

29   **Michigan:** Bay Harbor and Beyond 129
RECOMMENDED BY BRANDON TUCKER

30   **New Brunswick:** Algonquin Golf Club 135
RECOMMENDED BY THOMAS MCBROOM

31   **New Mexico:** Black Mesa Golf Club 139
RECOMMENDED BY BAXTER SPANN

32   **New York:** Montauk Downs 143
RECOMMENDED BY DAMON HACK

33   **New Zealand:** The Hills 147
RECOMMENDED BY SIR BOB CHARLES

34   **North Carolina:** Pinehurst No. 2 151
RECOMMENDED BY TIM MORAGHAN

35   **Ontario:** Devil's Paintbrush. 155
RECOMMENDED BY MIKE BELL

36   **Oregon:** Bandon Trails. 159
RECOMMENDED BY GRANT ROGERS

37   **Portugal:** Oitavos Dunes 165
RECOMMENDED BY DREW ROGERS

38   **Scotland–Dornoch:** Royal Dornoch 169
RECOMMENDED BY LORNE RUBENSTEIN

39   **Scotland–Islay:** The Machrie Golf Links 175
RECOMMENDED BY COLIN DALGLEISH

40   **Scotland–Machrihanish:** Machrihanish Golf Club. 179
RECOMMENDED BY BRIAN MORGAN

41   **Scotland–South Uist:** Askernish Old. 183
RECOMMENDED BY JOHN GARRITY

42   **South Africa:** Durban Country Club 187
RECOMMENDED BY GORDON TURNER

43   **South Carolina:** Kiawah Island (The Ocean Course) 193
RECOMMENDED BY HUNKI YUN

44   **Spain:** PGA Golf de Catalunya (Green) 196
RECOMMENDED BY GENE A. HOLLAND, JR.

45   **Thailand:** Blue Canyon (Canyon Course). 199
RECOMMENDED BY MIKE LARDNER

46   **United Arab Emirates:** Arabian Ranches 203
RECOMMENDED BY IAN BAKER-FINCH

47   **Uruguay:** Four Seasons Carmelo 208
RECOMMENDED BY BRIAN ROBBELOTH

48   **Vietnam:** Ho Chi Minh Golf Trail. 213
RECOMMENDED BY HAL PHILLIPS

49   **Wales:** A Welsh Sampler 216
RECOMMENDED BY JOHN HOPKINS

50   **Washington:** Chambers Bay Golf Course 219
RECOMMENDED BY BRUCE CHARLTON

ACKNOWLEDGMENTS

This book would not have been possible without the generous assistance of the expert golfers who shared their time and experiences to help bring these great golf venues to life. To these men and women, I offer the most heartfelt thanks. I would especially like to thank Jeff Wallach and Kevin Cook, who offered encouragement and made many introductions on my behalf. I also want to acknowledge the fine efforts of my agent, Stephanie Kip Rostan, editor, Jennifer Levesque, and designer, Anna Christian, who helped bring the book into being, along with copy editor Sylvia Karchmar and proofreader Elizabeth Norment.

Since I first picked up a golf club when I was sixteen years old, I've made many fine golfing friends, some of whom I can still defeat on occasion. This group includes Ken Matsumoto, Gary Smith, Howard Kyser, Peter "Jimi" Clough, Mike McDonough (I'm taking good care of the trophy, Mike!), Jeff Sang, Jerry Stein, Dave Sinise, Ed O'Brien, Don Ryder, Lee Galban, Andy and Peter Waugh, Dave Tegeler, Chris Bittenbender, Sloan Morris, Keith Carlson, Roberto Borgatti, Andrew Altman, and Paul Riffel. I look forward to many more days on the links with these friends and the new ones to be made on the first tee. These companions all understand that there's no performance on the first eighteen holes that can't be made a bit better by a brief stop at the nineteenth!

Lastly, I must thank my mom and dad for their constant encouragement, and the three ladies in my life—Deidre, Cassidy, and Annabel—for their generosity in time and spirit, which lets me slide away to the links so frequently. If only they could help me improve my game . . .

FOREWORD

I can tell you from personal experience that Chris Santella hits it long off the tee—and, okay, sometimes equally as wide. But you didn't buy this book because of Chris's "unique" swing; you bought it (or should buy it, if you're still browsing) because the guy can flat out write. He's basically a plus two handicap at writing. And researching.

Also, Chris knows the golf world, its dignitaries and debutantes. Here he's collected a group of experts in playing, managing, designing, and writing about golf courses who all admire Chris enough to have given up to him some of their favorite golf venues—many of which you won't be reading about on magazine "best course" lists. The names of some of these places are only whispered over drams of one-hundred-year-old malt whisky. Secret handshakes may well be involved. And albino priests.

As with all lists of both the golf and bucket variety, it's fun to stand in the bookstore (or better yet, to recline in your favorite leather club chair at home, after you've purchased the book) and flip through to see how many of these adventures you've checked off—or even heard of. The beauty of the volume you're now cradling is that the choices are quirky, highly personal, sometimes downright strange, and based as much on pure, unadulterated, unquantifiable experience as on golf politics, etiquette, or the accepted canon of so-called great courses. If you gathered the folks who consulted on this book and put them in a room together, hay would fly. Voices would most certainly be raised. Possibly, dancing would occur. What an utter pleasure it is to hear experts as diverse as Fred Funk and Gordon Dalgleish recommend courses as diverse and unexpected as El Cameleon (Mexico) and Spring City (China) for these pages. This, my friends, is a hardcover party!

I know from my own adventures as a golf and travel journalist for nearly twenty years that many of the courses you should play before you die (or before you simply get too tired and cranky) are in out-of-the-way locations. (I can recommend one in Nepal, for example, that doubles as a safari park.) Some are achingly gorgeous in design and/or setting (China's Jade Mountain Snow Dragon comes to mind). Others may boast some funky golf history (such as a rare layout designed by Alister Mackenzie's brother). All of the venues collected in these pages are here because one of our outspoken colleagues with insider knowledge took on the challenge and reached deep to offer up the truly rare and unusual. These might not be the familiar "classics" or (forgive me for even uttering the phrase) "hidden gems" (which are usually neither). You're unlikely to see the pros playing many of them on TV. But you might just enjoy some of the most memorable rounds of your life on these courses—chased by monkeys, or serenaded by a muezzin's call to prayer, or left speechless by the utter grace of your native caddie or distant mountains or the nearby sparkling sea splashing between you and the pin.

The thing that's so interesting about golf is not the par you nearly made on the 14th hole—and if you disagree, you can probably clear a barroom faster than a flaming whoop-ee cushion. What's interesting about golf is context, storytelling, the overall experience of traveling to and around a gorgeous piece of architected greenery. It's the miraculously absurd thing your best friend did on the practice tee, the shot hit from the second floor of the clubhouse. The view of rolling, rumpled topography beneath gathering stormclouds that leaves your heart pounding. It's *life*, is what I mean to say, and Chris Santella and his group of experts have described it in all its colors—not just green. Happy reading, and pass that bottle over here!

—Jeff Wallach

INTRODUCTION

I was a passionate (if terrible) golfer when I wrote *Fifty Places to Play Golf Before You Die*. In the four years since that book was published, my love for the game has only increased. I'm still terrible on the course (though not *quite* as terrible), but I believe that the increased understanding of the nuances of golf course design—and golf travel—that I've accumulated since working on that book have enabled me to better appreciate all the things that combine to make a memorable golf experience.

Thus it was with great enthusiasm that I embraced the chance to write another golf book—*Fifty More Places to Play Golf Before You Die*.

When I speak at clubs or do signings in bookstores, one of the first questions people ask is: "Did you get to visit all fifty places?" Sadly, I must answer "No." But the way I arrive at my list is perhaps the next best thing to visiting: I interview fifty people closely connected with the golf world about some of their favorite courses and experiences. These experts range from seasoned touring professionals (like Amy Alcott, Ian Baker-Finch, and Fred Funk) to golf journalists and photographers (like James Dodson, Jeff Wallach, and Brian Morgan) to golf course architects (like Robert von Hagge and Bob Harrison) to travel experts (like Gordon Dalgleish, Mike Lardner, and Joe Passov). I don't ask my interviewees to talk about "the best" course they've ever played; instead, I encourage people to talk about a course or experience that made a lasting impression on them or that's near and dear to their heart. It's my hope that in exploring how different golfers relate to different places and experiences, I'll be able to shed a tiny bit of light on the many diverse ways we come to appreciate the game. (To give a sense of the breadth of their golfing background, a bio of each individual is included after each essay.)

While this book collects fifty great golfing experiences, it by no means attempts to rank the courses discussed or the quality of the experiences each course affords. Such ranking is largely subjective, as the course that might be appealing to a golf course architecture critic might be unfathomable to an every-other-weekend player. In this spirit, courses are listed alphabetically by state or country.

In the hope that a few readers might embark on adventures of their own, I have provided some "If You Go" information at the end of each chapter. Though not exhaustive, it will give would-be travelers a starting point for planning their trip. I have also offered

some basic course information, including distances (from the championship tees, in each case), slope rating (if available), green fees, and contact information. Please do not interpret the listing of championship tee yardage as a recommendation that *you* play from those tees; an individual player will get the best sense of the experience a pro has on a course—and the idea that the architect had—by playing from the tee appropriate for his or her skills. I've also included some basic lodging options. Generally I've highlighted a chamber of commerce or tourism clearinghouse that lists a broad range of options suitable to a number of budgets and preferences. If my interviewees recommended a specific property, or if there's only one option in town, I've provided more specific information.

Like my first golf book, *Fifty More Places to Play Golf Before You Die* includes a handful of private courses. Some of my readers have protested their inclusion: Why do they want to read about Cypress Point if they can't ever play it? While I empathize with this sentiment, I felt that to be true to the book's premise—to let golf experts talk about their most memorable experiences—I would need to include a few of those private venues if they were special to the interviewee. And while it's not likely that you'll get an unsolicited invite to play Congressional, you never know who you might happen to sit next to on an airplane or in an Irish pub, or where a friendship struck up in conversation might lead. (On page 41, Joe Passov tells the tale of how *he* was invited to play Cypress Point—*it can happen!*)

While any round of golf is a good round in my estimation, a trip to a dream venue can create memories for a lifetime. I hope that this little book helps you tee off on a few adventures of your own.

OPPOSITE:
The Hills is set amidst the natural grandeur of the nearby Southern Alps on the South Island of New Zealand.
NEXT PAGE:
Pannonia Golf and Country Club in the Mariavolgy Valley outside Budapest is considered Hungary's finest course.

The Destinations

JASPER PARK GOLF CLUB

RECOMMENDED BY **Bob Weeks**

The promotional literature of the Fairmont Jasper Park Lodge includes the following guest-book entry from 1925:

> A New York man reaches heaven, and as he passes the gate, St. Peter says, "I am sure you will like it." A Pittsburgh man follows and St. Peter says, "It will be a great change for you." Finally, there comes a man from Jasper Park Lodge. "I am afraid," says St. Peter, "that you will be disappointed."

The entry, penned by Sherlock Holmes' creator, Sir Arthur Conan Doyle, certainly speaks to the incredible mountain scenery of the valley where the Fairmont Jasper Park Lodge sits. We can only guess what Doyle, an avid golfer, would've written had he had the chance to play the golf course, which opened the following year.

"When I first played the Jasper Park Golf Club, I had the overwhelming feeling that it might just be the perfect golf experience," Bob Weeks began. "The sun was shining, the scenery was incredible, the layout of the course was great. I recall thinking that if a golf nirvana existed, this was it; it was as close to perfection as I'd experienced. And I don't even remember how I played!"

The golf course at Jasper came to be thanks in part to the Canadian National Railroad. As the railroads pushed west across Canada in the late 1800s, great hotels were built along the way—a lure to put paying passengers on the train. To the south, in Banff National Park, Canadian National's rival—Canadian Pacific Railway—constructed a golf course (including nine holes routed by Donald Ross) to complement the Banff Springs Hotel. Not to be outdone, Canadian National's Sir Harry Thornton commissioned Stanley Thompson, already a rising star in golf course architecture circles, to build a grand course

OPPOSITE:
The view from
behind the green
on Jasper's 16th,
with the sparkling
waters of Lac
Beauvert and
the Canadian
Rockies in the
background.

in the valley near crystal clear Lac Beauvert, adjoining the Jasper Park Lodge. It was not long before the Jasper Park Golf Club was praised as one of the greatest golf courses in the world.

Bob first visited Jasper in the early 1990s. "Being Canadian, I'd long heard about the historic Stanley Thompson courses in the Rockies, though I didn't know what to expect," he continued. "For starters, the drive into Jasper is stunning for a guy like me who grew up in the city. At every turn, there's a remarkable mountain vista. You're in a national park, and there are elk, mountain goat, and bear walking along the road. The lodge is circled by little cabins. From the outside, you don't expect them to be fancy, but they are, each with a cozy fireplace. When I made it to the course, I was expecting it to be difficult; in the nineties, the ethos was that a good course had to be difficult. That wasn't the experience at all at Jasper. It's not an easy track, but the playability is tremendous. Thanks to the nuances of Thompson's design, you experience it differently each time you play, yet you don't feel beaten up. Every time it's enjoyable."

Stanley Thompson's brilliance as a golf course architect is not widely recognized beyond Canada, but in recent years his work has been enjoying increased scrutiny and acclaim from design aficionados. Thompson devotees may have difficulty reaching consensus on naming his finest design—Highland Links, Banff Springs, Capilano, and St. Georges, along with Jasper, all rank high on the list—though no lesser luminaries than Alister MacKenzie and George Thomas placed Jasper amongst their favorites . . . anywhere. The course beautifully illustrates two of Thompson's signature design traits—an ingenious integration of course features with the natural surroundings, and elegant, imaginative bunkering. "From some of the tee decks, your driving target is a mountain peak," Bob described. "When you closely investigate the mounding behind the greens, you'll notice that they're a perfect replication of the mountains in the background. Every time I go around the course, new subtleties reveal themselves. I always come away thinking that Thompson was a genius—especially when you consider the kind of earthmoving equipment that was available in the 1920s." The bunkering at Jasper brings the notion of sand hazards to high art. On the 10th hole (called "The Maze," thanks to its eleven bunkers), one of the bunkers is in the shape of an octopus; another is the shape of the constellation Boötes Arcturus. "Thompson is said to have done much of his routing at night, riding around the grounds on horseback," Jasper's director of golf Alan Carter explained. "One of those rides inspired the Boötes Arcturus bunkers."

There are too many defining moments at Jasper Park to give each its proper due—the vista of the "Old Man" mountain formation on the par 5 2nd hole, the blind tee shots on the par 4 3rd and 8th holes, the three-hole jaunt onto the peninsula that juts into Lac Beauvert on the 14th through 16th. For an appreciation of Stanley Thompson's design prowess (and sense of humor), one must linger at the par 3 9th, dubbed "Cleopatra." The name is derived from the hole's backdrop, Pyramid Mountain, and from the fact that it once took the general shape of a woman reclining on her back. The hole measures 231 yards from the tips, though with an elevation drop of eighty feet, it plays much shorter. Seven bunkers adorn the hole, and three of these are well in front, though they appear closer from the tee. These three bunkers were missing from Cleopatra's initial incarnation; instead, there were two mounds that more than suggested a woman's breasts.

The story goes that the Canadian National Railway owed Thompson half of his fee for laying out Jasper, and that he knew very well that Cleopatra would get the railroad's attention. It worked. On Jasper's opening day, Thompson accompanied Sir Harry Thornton on his first round. When they reached the 9th, Thompson reported that Canadian National's president simply stared down at the hole—and, in Thompson's words, "blew a gasket." Cleopatra's curves were soon replaced with the fronting bunkers, though not before Thompson received the balance of his fee.

BOB WEEKS is editor of *SCOREGolf*, Canada's leading golf magazine and website.

If You Go

▶ **Getting There:** Jasper National Park is almost equidistant from Calgary and Edmonton (about five hours' drive), though the ride from Calgary is stunning—one of the world's great drives. Calgary is served by most major carriers.

▶ **Course Information:** The par 71 course plays 6,663 yards from the back tees, with a slope of 124. Tee times (780-852-6090; www.fairmontgolf.com) are required.

▶ **Accommodations:** The Fairmont Jasper Park Lodge (866-540-4454; www.fairmont.com/jasper) has 446 guestrooms, each with an air of rustic elegance. Many outdoor activities are available. During high season, rooms begin at around $500 CAD.

TALKING STICK (SOUTH COURSE)

RECOMMENDED BY **Tim Greenwell**

There are a number of wonderful golf courses around the world that live perpetually in the shadow of their more celebrated neighbors. Pacific Grove Golf Club, just north of Pebble Beach, and Old Prestwick, across the way from the Aisla Course at Turnberry, are a couple that come to mind. For Tim Greenwell, a third is Talking Stick South.

"The South Course has been the redheaded stepchild of the Talking Stick facility since it opened in 1997," Tim began. "The North course got all the accolades—it still does. Yet the South is a spectacular track, too. It's a much more traditional design, with trees along many of the fairways and less aggressively bunkered greens. It's certainly challenging for a good player, but it's the kind of course where a beginning player can learn and gain confidence. My wife, Jeane, learned to play golf there with me, and that's one reason Talking Stick South is special to me."

The Talking Stick golf complex is situated on the Salt River Pima-Maricopa Indian Community, which borders the golf-rich city of Scottsdale, Arizona. (Scottsdale boasts more golf courses per capita than any other city in the world, with some 200 courses for approximately 240,000 citizens; indeed, the *Robb Report* named Scottsdale "America's Best Place to Live for Golf.") The complex differs from many facilities in greater Scottsdale in several ways: first, it's very convenient to downtown; second, the courses are not ringed by houses, despite the proximity to the city center; and finally, both are a pronounced departure from the desert golf most associate with Arizona, where players are compelled to advance the ball from one ribbon of green to the next over vast expanses of Sonoran wasteland. (Scottsdale is widely considered the birthplace of desert-style target golf, ushered in by Lyle Anderson and Jack Nicklaus with the unveiling of Desert Highlands in 1981.) The 400-acre site where the two courses would take shape was flat and rather nondescript when work began. In keeping with their minimalist design philosophy, architects Bill Coore and Ben Crenshaw chose not to move tons of dirt around; yet they still were able to create two spectacular, though very different tracks. The inland-links North—devoid of water, and for the most part trees, but ingeniously bunkered—certainly speaks to the style of courses that Messrs. Coore and Crenshaw have built their daring reputation on. But the notion of building a traditional tree-lined course in Scottsdale is perhaps the most subversive and unexpected thing they could have done. (More than 4,500 cottonwoods, eucalyptus, and sycamores were planted along the fairways at the South to lend it an Eastern Establishment look.) Despite the trees, the South Course has a minimalist feeling of its own.

The name Talking Stick, incidentally, refers to the Pima people's traditional calendar stick, which was used to record significant events in the course of the year.

"There's a herd of wild mustangs that call the Salt River Pima-Maricopa Reservation home," Tim continued. "When construction of the courses started, they could barely get grass to grow, as the horses would wander in and eat it. Barbed-wire fences had to be erected in part to keep the horses out. When Coore and Crenshaw started work on the South Course, they incorporated the fence into the layout of several of the holes. Instead of it being an eyesore, the fence became a feature of the course. If you're a lover of golf architecture, you appreciate touches like this. The horses are still out on the perimeter, and you'll sometimes see them running about. There's not a home for miles and miles, and it can be eerily quiet. At twilight, you can hear the coyotes howling."

Golf may not be the first thing that springs to mind when considering Scottsdale in the summertime; after all, mid-day temperatures can exceed 110 degrees. Yet Tim makes a compelling case for considering a mid-afternoon, mid-August round. "Summer play in Arizona might be one of the best values in the golf world. The courses are in the best shape of the year, there are big price breaks, and not many people are doing it." About the heat: "The temperature tends to peak at 3 P.M.; you can feel it start to diminish by 3:30. Many golfers will queue up to tee off at 4 when twilight rates start. I like to head out at 2:30 to get a jump on the crowds. By 4 P.M., I'm on the 7th hole, and can see the groups all lined up at the first tee. I've always found that if a course has treed fairways, it's going to be a bit cooler. That's certainly the case on the South Course; in fact, there's not a single hole where you can't find some shade. Playing in the heat is great from a health standpoint. I drink lots of water on the course, two or three gallons. It flushes out your system.

By the end of the summer, I weigh ten pounds less. I haven't dieted or exercised any more—the only thing I do differently is play golf in the heat."

The way you play a certain hole as your golf game evolves can be as good a determinant as any of your progress. For Tim, the story of his wife's development is best told from the tees on the par 5 16th at Talking Stick South. "From the back tee, it's about 550 yards; from the Ladies' Tee, 440 yards," Tim said. "The hole plays to a dogleg left, and there's a creek that runs along the right side of the fairway, coming into play at about 300 yards. It runs along the fairway until about 50 yards in front of the green; at that point, it cuts in front of the green. I love the hole, as it comes late in the round when I'm hankering for a birdie, and it plays to my game—a slight hook. It's reachable in two for long hitters, especially if you can get your second shot into the air.

"When we started playing Talking Stick eight years ago, it would take Jeane four strokes just to get to the water. Now, if she hits a good drive, she can clear the water in two—and she expects to do it. I can still remember the first time she was over in two shots. For her, it was the golf equivalent of breaking the four-minute mile."

TIM GREENWELL is senior vice president, sales and marketing for Troon Golf, where he's responsible for the development of all advertising, sales, marketing, and public relations strategies for the company and its facilities. He has over eighteen years' marketing experience in the golf industry, including positions with the Arizona Golf Association, the USGA, and the PGA of America.

If You Go

OPPOSITE:
Despite its desert
locale, Talking
Stick South
has a parkland
feel one might
expect to find in
the suburbs of
New York.

▶ **Getting There:** Talking Stick Golf Club is in Scottsdale, roughly thirty minutes from Sky Harbor Airport in Phoenix, which is served by most major carriers.

▶ **Course Information:** Par 71 Talking Stick (480-860-2221; www.talkingstickgolfclub.com) plays 6,833 yards from the black tees, with a slope rating of 129. Green fees vary from $110 to $130, depending on the season you visit.

▶ **Accommodations:** The Scottsdale Convention and Visitors Bureau (800-782-1117; www.scottsdalecvb.com) provides an overview of lodging options. Countless packages are available in this golf mecca.

GOLF CLUB AT KENNEDY BAY

RECOMMENDED BY **Spencer Schaub**

"If Kennedy Bay were in suburban America, it could draw up to 400 rounds a day—it's the kind of course that people would sleep in their cars in the parking lot to play," Spencer Schaub began. "But being forty minutes south of Perth on the west coast of Australia, it sees very little play. This is a boon to those who make it here, as it's a great conceptual design on a wonderful piece of land."

As a descriptive term, "links" has become one of the most used—and, in some learned opinions, most *misused*—descriptors in golf. For some, it's enough to have a golf course situated in sight of a body of water to have it qualify as a links. For others, a tract of treeless land—no matter how far from the sea—will suffice. Kennedy Bay bills itself as a true links experience, with the substitution of Australian bushland shrubbery for Scottish gorse, and the inviting Indian Ocean for the chilly North Sea. Given its sand-dune base, the presence of 115 pot bunkers (small but devilishly difficult to extract one-self from), and fairways that give bounce and roll—not to mention the absence of flora beyond the bush—Kennedy Bay offers up an honest approximation of the links experi-ence, with an Australasian flair (more on that later). The course was designed by archi-tects Michael Coate and Roger Mackay along with British Open champion and native Aussie Ian Baker-Finch.

True to its linksy nature, play at Kennedy Bay is heavily influenced by the wind—namely, the Fremantle Doctrine. (Fremantle, sailing aficionados will recall, was the site of the 1987 America's Cup Race, where the United States wrested the cup back from Australia under Dennis Conner's command.) "It has always been my experience that when you play the first nine holes out, you're straight into the wind," Spencer said. "As the Fremantle Doctrine kicks in toward afternoon, you're playing back into the wind again. It seemed as if there were a ghost living out there in the dunes, signaling the wind to reverse direction as soon as I made the turn. I always thought that if I ever met the ghost, I'd tell him how unfair this is."

A number of holes at Kennedy Bay stand out. On the shorter side of the spectrum, there are two notable par 3s—the 6th and the 16th. Measuring 213 yards from the tips, the 6th plays to an elevated green with an open front for run-up shots. Many consider the 16th, which plays a modest 150 yards, to be the finest hole on the course. Played into the prevailing wind, the center of this narrow, steeply sloped green is blocked by a pot bunker; two other bunkers wait in back to punish overzealous hitters. On the longer side of the spectrum, the par 5 4th hole, measuring 568 yards, will linger in your memory, thanks in large part to the humongous bunker that stretches across the right side of the fairway, 100-odd yards from the green; you'll want to think carefully about your second shot! (Perhaps Baker-Finch was thinking about one of his outings at St. Andrews when fashioning this replica of the Hell Bunker from the Old Course's 14th hole.)

"There are some big dunes that rest between the edge of the course and the Indian Ocean," Spencer continued, "and being a green American visitor, I felt the need to peer over the edge. As I climbed over, I realized that there was a beach on the other side. As I climbed down in my golf togs, it was soon apparent that it was a nude beach. It's an image I won't soon forget—me in my golf clothes, standing amidst a group of naked people. From that day on, whenever we had visitors to the course, I'd ask them to have a look at the beach."

For Spencer, the attractions of Kennedy Bay extend far beyond the fairways. "My career in the golf industry has taken me to live in a number of places outside of my native United States, and has allowed me to have other life experiences beyond golf," he continued. "My stay at Kennedy Bay was incredibly rewarding. You're less than an hour away from Fremantle, a popular seaside resort town for Western Australia residents, and the Margaret River region is just an hour south. Margaret River is one of Western Australia's premier wine growing regions, renowned for its Cabernets. There's excellent cuisine, too. There are also some great waves off the coast here, if you want to try your hand at surfing. With a visit to Kennedy Bay, you can have a great Western Australia experience for four or five days, plus a great golf experience." For those hoping to supplement the golf portion of a Western Australia adventure, other well-regarded courses include Joondalup Resort Country Club, Novotel Vines Resort, and Secret Harbour Golf Links.

As any golfer knows, there are a number of good reasons to keep the ball on the fairway, not the least of which is to ensure a good lie for your approach shot. At Kennedy Bay, Spencer Schaub learned a more compelling reason to hit it straight—his personal safety. "Australia is home to three of the deadliest snakes in the world, and I'm the first to run—very fast—when I see one of those. On one of the first occasions that I played Kennedy Bay, I was in the company of the director of golf. I pushed the ball a bit to the right, and he said 'Your ball is a bit off the beaten path, Spencer. You probably don't want to go crunching in there after it, as we have some pretty big snakes here.' He didn't have to tell me again. For the next ten times I hit a drive, if I wasn't on the short stuff, I'd never go in looking for my ball—even if I was only ten yards off the fairway.

"The presence of large venomous snakes provides an excellent incentive to hit the ball straight."

SPENCER SCHAUB has worked in the golf industry most of his adult life. He began his career at Eagle Ridge Inn and Resort as tournament coordinator/head professional. From there he took on his first international assignment as operations manager for Troon Golf Australia. Following his time in Australia, Spencer became part of the pre-opening and current golf operations team at The Grove in England. Spencer is a Class A member of the PGA and was named the 2004 Troon Golf Associate of the Year. He holds a business degree from Ferris State University in Big Rapids, Michigan.

If You Go

▶ **Getting There:** Kennedy Bay is forty minutes south of Perth, which is served by many major carriers, including Air New Zealand (800-262-1234; www.airnewzealand.com) British Airways (800-247-9297; www.britishairways.com), and Qantas Air (800-227-4500; www.qantas.com).

▶ **Course Information:** Kennedy Bay Golf Club (+62 08 9524 5333: www.kennedybay.com.au) plays 7,021 yards to a par 72. Green fees are $65 AUD.

▶ **Accommodations:** Spencer recommends staying in nearby Fremantle, a popular getaway for Aussies. Contact the Fremantle Visitors Centre (+61 8 9431; www.fremantlewa.au.com) or Tourism Western Australia (www.westernaustralia.com).

BARNBOUGLE DUNES

RECOMMENDED BY **Michael Clayton**

Links-style golf has been successfully imported from the coastlines of Scotland and Ireland to points as far afield as Lake Michigan (Whistling Straits) and the Oregon coast (Bandon Dunes). Perhaps its most unlikely export—and certainly one of its most successful—has been to the isolated coast of northern Tasmania, in the shape of Barnbougle Dunes.

"A young entrepreneur named Greg Ramsay had seen the land at Barnbougle, which belonged to a potato farmer and businessman named Richard Sattler," Michael Clayton began. "Greg had worked as a caddie at St. Andrews, had a love for links golf, and recognized the property's potential. He kept ringing Richard about the sand dunes on the edge of his property. I think Richard, who knew absolutely nothing about golf, thought Greg was a bit mad, but eventually he gave in to his enthusiasm and persistence, saying 'If you can raise the money, you can build the course.' Greg asked Bruce Hepner (from Tom Doak's design firm) and me to look at the land and read us the 'This design will make you guys famous' speech. He was certainly right about the land, and my design partners (John Sloan and Bruce Grant), along with Tom's company, signed on. There was some question about the viability of the project from a business perspective. Many felt it was too far away, too windy—too this, too that—and that there was nothing like such a project in Australia, both in terms of the site and the fact that this course would be open to the public. Mike Keiser (who'd overcome many of the same objections at Bandon Dunes) soon stepped in and lent his support. The local government was very supportive, and Richard agreed to proceed. By 2003, work had begun."

And by 2006, just two years after opening, Barnbougle took its place in *Golf* magazine's "Top 100 in the World" list.

The Australian state of Tasmania lies some 150 miles south across the Bass Strait from Melbourne; it's sometimes called "the island off the island." Tasmania is cooler than mainland Australia, and a bit wetter. With its mountainous terrain and slower pace of life, it may seem to have more in common with New Zealand than Australia, especially to Western perceptions. With its rolling dunes, marram grass, and breathtaking ocean vistas, Barnbougle could easily be mistaken for Ballybunion on Ireland's west coast—with wider fairways. "Barnbougle is not a difficult course," Michael continued. "Some of the fairways are amazingly wide—eighty or ninety yards. Still, it's amazing how crookedly players can hit it when they don't feel constrained by the trees that they're accustomed to have lining the fairways—especially when the ball gets into the wind. If there's one complaint some people have about Barnbougle, it's that the course is too windy. It's true that it can be windy at times, but no more so than Royal Birkdale or Shinnecock Hills. After all, it's the wind that formed the land that makes the course worth playing. In reality, the course is routed so the longest holes are with the prevailing wind; with the exception of the last few holes, only the shorter holes are against it."

One of the shorter holes that captivates Michael Clayton (and most visitors) is the 4th, which measures a scant 296 yards from the tips. On days when the wind is down, the hole is certainly in reach, though one must carry a gaping bunker that's twenty feet deep—and reputed to be the largest sand trap in the Southern Hemisphere. "If you can carry it at 220 yards or so, you can kick it down on to the green," Michael advised. For those of us less able to depend on such a carry, he advises to play to the side of the fairway that's opposite the day's pin placement. The 446-yard 8th is another great hole, though it has sparked some controversy among regulars. "It's a long par 4 with a dune in the middle, essentially splitting the fairway," Michael explained. "You have to choose which path you'll take off your drive. It's a harder play to the left as there's more carry and less room, but you have a much better perspective of the hole as you're higher up. It's a big two-shot hole however you look at it. Perhaps the fact that it arouses debate shows that it works as a golf hole."

"One of the things I love about Barnbougle is the relaxed atmosphere of the place," Michael said. "There are none of the restrictions or stratifications that are so much a part of the Australian private club scene—it's very friendly, and guests feel none of the intimidation that public golfers experience when visiting a private club. A bit of this comes from Tasmania's rural character, the rest from the fact that Richard was unacquainted

OPPOSITE:

Barnbougle
Dunes brings a
wee bit of the old
country to the
northern coast
of Tasmania.

with many of the formalized customs of golf. He didn't want rules like 'no jeans,' and there aren't any such rules. People come to experience the beauty of the place and the great game that the course affords. An added pleasure is the chance to mingle with the people who live here. At night, the clubhouse turns into the local restaurant, and many non-golfers come in for dinner or a pint. To me, it's wonderfully refreshing. If the same course was in Melbourne, guests wouldn't have the chance to meet and mingle with the course's staff or neighboring farmers."

MICHAEL CLAYTON turned professional in 1981 after a very successful amateur career, which included winning the Australian Amateur Championship in 1978 and the Victorian Amateur Championship in 1977 and 1981. After turning professional, he devoted his time to the Australian and European tours, winning a number of tournaments, including the Victorian Open Championship in 1982 and 1989, the Korean Open in 1984, the Tasmanian Open in 1984, the Australian Matchplay in 1991, the Coolum Classic in 1994, and the Heineken Classic in 1994. As well as being a talented professional golfer, Mike is a journalist, writing regular golfing articles for the *Melbourne Age* newspaper and *Australian Golfing* magazine. He is also an accomplished golf course architect, with designs at Ranfurlie, Barnbougle Dunes, and St. Andrews Beach (the latter two with Tom Doak) to his credit.

If You Go

▶ **Getting There:** Barnbougle Dunes is in the Tasmanian town of Bridport, roughly one-and-a-half hours from the airport in Launceston, which is served from Sydney and Melbourne by Qantas Air (800-227-4500; www.qantas.com).

▶ **The Course:** Barnbougle Dunes plays 6,724 yards from the tips to a par 71. Green fees are $98 AUD for 18, $120 AUD for all-day play. Barnbougle is a walk-only course, unless guests have a medical certificate to verify an illness or disability.

▶ **Accommodations:** Barnbougle has comfortable cottages on the property with views of the sea and the course. Rates begin at $160 AUD for two; reservations can be made at www.barnbougledunes.com.au.

CAPILANO GOLF AND COUNTRY CLUB

RECOMMENDED BY **Doug Roxburgh**

"My most vivid memory of Capilano is my very first visit," four-time Canadian Amateur champion Doug Roxburgh reminisced. "I was fourteen years old and caddying in a tournament for my instructor, Jack Westover, and the game was at Capilano. It was a dreary day, and as we drove up toward the course, the clouds got lower and lower—and then suddenly, there to the right was the course. When I came off Capilano that day, I could remember every hole. It was the first Stanley Thompson course I'd ever seen. I came back the following year to play in the British Columbia Junior Boys Championship—it was a real luxury for us boys to play such a course. I've played many events there since, including the BC Amateur and on the Canadian team in the World Amateurs. The scenery—especially on a clear day—is just spectacular. And any day, it's the kind of course that challenges you to use every club in the bag, from every possible lie—uphill, downhill, and sidehill."

Capilano clings to the southern face of Hollyburn Mountain in West Vancouver, across the Burrard Inlet from Vancouver proper. ("Capilano" is the anglicized form of a name held by First Nations men of mixed Squamish and Musqueam heritage; the course is just west of the Capilano River.) Players teeing off on the glorious par 4 6th will note that the hole's trajectory aligns smartly with Lion's Gate Bridge (more on number 6 later). The realization of Capilano was closely connected to the completion of the bridge. A shrewd entrepreneur named A.J.T. Taylor —well connected both in Vancouver and England—was able to negotiate very favorable terms for the purchase of 6,000 acres of West Vancouver property (including 160 acres for a golf course) for a group of investors that included the Guinness family (of stout-brewing fame). To make these homesites—and the golf course he had long imagined—a feasible suburban retreat, he needed a bridge to the city. Through

diligent arm-twisting, Taylor eventually got the bridge signed off on by the Canadian prime minister. What was then the world's second-largest suspension bridge (the Golden Gate Bridge was the longest) officially opened in 1939, the same year that Capilano's grand clubhouse opened its doors. (Play had begun on the course in 1937.)

Taylor had not waited for approval of the bridge project before laying plans for the golf course that he hoped would draw well-heeled homebuyers across Burrard Inlet. In 1931, he hired Stanley Thompson to wrest a course from the heavily forested mountainside; Thompson accepted the assignment before ever seeing the site. (Upon visiting West Vancouver the following winter, Thompson was quite satisfied with what Mother Nature had given him to work with, and recognized that Capilano had potential to be perhaps the finest work of his career.) Known as the "Toronto Terror"—perhaps because of his proclivity for alcohol, perhaps for his competitive nature on the golf course—Thompson made periodic visits west from his offices in New York, returning east to create plasticene molds of the holes he envisioned.

Drama seemed to follow Thompson, and on one visit to Capilano shortly before the course would open, a small design tweak earned him the attention of the West Vancouver police. The story goes that Thompson looked down the first fairway and declared that some trees to the left of the hole were blocking a view of Burrard Inlet and the Vancouver skyline. When told that the trees were not on golf course property, Thompson instructed his crew to remove them nonetheless. A local constable soon caught up with Thompson at the course, and informed the architect that he would have to come down to the station to explain himself. Thompson acquiesced, but before going, he asked the policeman to accompany him to the clubhouse site at the top of the property. Once there, he pointed down the first fairway and is said to have exclaimed, "Isn't this the most glorious view you've ever seen in your life? If we didn't cut those trees, you would never have been able to see this view." The officer acknowledged that it was a fantastic view and left Thompson to his devices—though not before imploring him not to cut down any more trees that were not on club property.

The first hole at Capilano not only sets the stage for the rest of the day, but also encapsulates some of the qualities that make the course stand out. A short par 5 (for members) and a longer par 4 (for tourney players), the 448-yard 1st plays sharply downhill, and offers the aforementioned view of Vancouver; it's fittingly named Hathstauwk, Squamish for "beautiful view." Those hitting even a moderately long drive have a great chance to

OPPOSITE:

The Vancouver skyline peeks through the trees from the tee on the par 5 5th.

reach the green in two, but they'll want to beware of—and marvel at—the handsome Thompson bunkers that flank the large green. These characteristics—the vistas, the use of the steep terrain (there's a variance of nearly 500 feet from the high point on the course to the low point), and Thompson's elegant bunkering (designed to reprimand poor or risky shots but save players, as often as possible, from the more punitive rebuke of lost balls) all make Capilano shine.

As Hathstauwk perfectly sets the tone for a round at Capilano, the par 5 18th—Wha-multchasum—provides a fitting close. At 556 yards and steadily uphill—with a blind second shot, and potentially a blind third to a raised green guarded by ominous bunkers at its base—this is a three-shot hole for just about everyone. Capilano's regal Tudor club-house rests to the right of the putting surface, a reminder that there will soon be an opportunity to toast one of the finest outings Canadian golf has to offer.

DOUG ROXBURGH is director of high-performance player development for the Royal Canadian Golf Association. A member of the Canadian Golf Hall of Fame, Doug has won the Canadian Amateur Championship four times and the British Columbia Amateur Championship thirteen times. He has represented Canada a dozen times in international play, and is an enthusiastic supporter of junior golf.

If You Go

▶ **Getting There:** Capilano is roughly twenty minutes from downtown Vancouver, across the Lion's Gate Bridge in West Vancouver.

▶ **Course Information:** Capilano Golf Club (604-925-4653; www.capilanogolf.com) plays 6,495 yards to a par 72; it has a slope rating of 125. The private club is rumored to have one of Canada's longest waiting lists for membership.

▶ **Accommodations:** Vancouver is a delightful city where British and Asian influences rub up alongside each other against the backdrop of mountains and sea. The Greater Vancouver Visitors and Convention Bureau (www.tourismvancouver.com) list the city's broad array of lodging options.

RUSTIC CANYON GOLF COURSE

RECOMMENDED BY **Geoff Shackelford**

For serious students of golf course design, the chance to try their hand at sculpting a course of their own poses both a once-in-a-lifetime opportunity and a potential risk—the risk coming from exposing one's work to the slings and arrows of those whose work you've critiqued in the past. In 2000, just such an opportunity came to noted golf historian and author Geoff Shackelford.

"As long as I can remember, I've drawn golf holes and have been fascinated by both the game and its architectural aspects," Geoff Shackelford began. "When I finished college, I had the chance to travel to many of the great courses in Scotland with my dad, who worked with American Golf. I also studied George C. Thomas, Jr.'s *Golf Architecture in America* cover to cover. This propelled my writing career, and I started doing books on golf architecture. I happened to meet an architect from Pennsylvania named Gil Hanse. It turned out he had read a few of my books, and he said in an offhand manner, "If a project ever arises and you want to work together, I'd love to do it." In 2000, that project materialized; a friend of my father was developing a property called Rustic Canyon in Ventura County, north of Los Angeles. A number of developers and architects toured the site—dry, hilly scrub land, for the most part—and came away feeling it wasn't much good for golf. When I walked the land I thought that it could make a remarkable golf course."

Soon after his first walk-through, Geoff teamed up with Gil Hanse and Jim Wagner and began laying the plans for Rustic Canyon. He spent about 200 days walking the site, trying to envision the routing. These exacting efforts resulted in a fine example of what Geoff terms "rustic golf"—an offshoot of classic links fused with an aesthetic inspired by the look and feel of certain Australian courses. "Golf in America has become extremely lush, often greatly at odds with the environment," Geoff continued. "Our goal was to

place the course in the midst of the terrain we had to work with, rather than reshape the land to meld with our vision of what the course might be. In Southern California, we have a dry climate, and in the region of Ventura County where Rustic Canyon is, there are many ranches. We tried to incorporate the feel of the surrounding ranch land into the layout—split-level fences, rugged, untamed terrain outside of the immediate field of play. I've described it as rustic golf, but it could also be called ranch golf. There are some severe contours and other quirky features on the course, but nearly all of them were there when we started; we just followed the natural characteristics of the land. Some players will initially reject such design elements, sensing they are manmade. If they understand that these elements are natural, they're more willing to accept them."

The many appeals of Rustic Canyon do not seize the first-time visitor upon arrival. There's no crashing surf, lonely cypresses, snowcapped mountains, or dazzling fountains. Instead, there's a *seemingly* flat expanse of land in pleasing, if unremarkable, Happy Camp Canyon. The greens of the fairways and putting surfaces stand in sharp contrast to the earth tones of the native vegetation—much of it sage scrub—that's been left as undisturbed as possible. A dry wash bisects the property, and figures frequently in the course of play. Though it may seem flat, there's actually an elevation change of 243 feet from the 13th green at the top of the canyon to the 4th green at the southwest end of the course. Geoff pointed out that putts tend to break in this direction.

Geoff Shackelford and his fellow conspirators are well versed in the design tenets of the golden age of golf architecture, a canon that preaches playability for the less gifted golfer and encourages strategic shot selection for the low-handicapper. At Rustic Canyon, you'll find a thoughtful application of those principles. Wide fairways provide even directionally challenged drivers a decent chance of hitting paydirt. Though the fairways are wide, there are certainly quadrants that provide birdie hunters with more expedient access to the pin; precision is not required, but it sure helps! ("Many regulars at Rustic Canyon will drive slowly onto the course to scout out the pin placements," Geoff added, "as this will influence which side of the fairway you'll want to play to.") In a nod toward a links sensibility, many holes at Rustic Canyon have generous entrances to the greens blanketed in the same bent grass as the putting surfaces, in hopes of encouraging players to play the bump and run shots that are so much a part of old country golf.

For many golf design buffs, there's nothing quite so pleasing as a well-conceived short par 4, the kind of hole that tempts you to swing away, yet has potential to punish those

OPPOSITE:
With native grasses left intact off the fairways, Rustic Canyon blends in beautifully with the dry hillsides of Ventura County.

who throw caution to the wind and err. Rustic Canyon has three such holes—the 3rd, the 7th, and the 12th. At 315, 330, and 340 yards, respectively, with sprawling fairways and relatively few hazards, all hold out the promise of easy birdies. Yet less fortunate outcomes are more often the case. The 3rd and the 7th offer different approach options, and it generally takes a few plays of these holes to find the plan of attack that best suits your game (and confidence level). The 12th seems absurdly straightforward, but things aren't always as they seem. "Number 12 was inspired by the 10th hole at Riviera Country Club, though it looks nothing like it," Geoff explained. "It plays to a massively wide fairway with an open fronted green that's slightly to the left. It's tempting to try to drive it, though if you lay up, you have a much better chance of making four. After all the times I've played it, I still get suckered into trying to get on in one . . . and I make a six!"

GEOFF SHACKELFORD is the author of ten books, including *Lines of Charm: Brilliant and Irreverent Quotes, Notes, and Anecdotes from Golf's Golden Age Architects*; *The Future of Golf: How Golf Lost Its Way and How to Get It Back*; *Grounds for Golf: The History and Fundamentals of Golf Course Design*; *Alister MacKenzie's Cypress Point Club*; and *The Golden Age of Golf Design*. His writing has also appeared in every significant golf magazine; in 2004/2005, *The Golfer* named him one of modern golf's ten most influential writers. Geoff is currently a contributing editor to *Golfdom* magazine, where he writes a monthly column as well as feature stories. He is collaborating on other designs in Cabo San Lucas, Vancouver Island, and Valentine, Nebraska.

If You Go

▶ **Getting There:** Rustic Canyon is in Moorpark, California, roughly an hour north of Los Angeles, and midway between Los Angeles and Santa Barbara.

▶ **Course Information:** Rustic Canyon (805-530-0221; www.rusticcanyongolfcourse. com) plays 6,988 yards from the black tees to a par 72. Green fees are $37 to $60.

▶ **Accommodations:** There are many lodging options in the area, including the Best Western Posada Royale (800-994-4884; www.posadaroyale.com) in nearby Simi Valley and the Four Seasons at Westlake Village (800-819-5053; www.fourseasons.com/westlakevillage) in Thousand Oaks.

CYPRESS POINT CLUB

RECOMMENDED BY **Joe Passov**

As a golf travel and architecture expert and course rankings editor for *Golf* magazine, Joe Passov has played a few golf courses (over 1,200 and counting) in his time. When asked to name a favorite, he barely missed a beat: "Cypress Point. It's head and shoulders above everything else I've ever experienced. I've gotten to play it twice, and I'm still wonderstruck by the place. My heart goes faster every time I drive near it—it's holy ground."

For the few who have had the good fortune to tread upon its sacrosanct fairways, mere superlatives hardly do justice to Cypress Point's allure. As Golf Club Atlas (an online compendium of erudite reviews of international golf course architecture) notes,

> Everyone, literally everyone, gushes over Cypress Point . . . One of the author's major contentions is that if a great architect is given a great piece of land, then a great course will follow. And at Cypress, the greatest architect was given his greatest piece of property, after the original architect, Seth Raynor, passed away.

The "greatest piece of property" is in the town of Pebble Beach (yes, there is also a town of that name), west of the much better known (and infinitely more accessible) home of the AT&T National Pro-Am; indeed, it's the most westerly course on the Monterey peninsula, bordering the Pacific. The "greatest architect" alluded to above is, of course, Dr. Alister MacKenzie, a Cambridge-trained physician of Scotch descent who, while serving in the Boer War, had his first inspiration for golf course design after observing the Boer's concealed trenches. Though said to be a player of only middling ability, MacKenzie found comfort in the game and advocated participation for his patients: "How frequently have I,

39

with great difficulty, persuaded patients who were never off my doorstep to take up golf, and how rarely, if ever, have I seen them in my consulting rooms again!"

Like Pine Valley outside of Philadelphia, Cypress Point is notoriously difficult for *anyone* to get on to play. Yet small miracles do happen, as Joe Passov recounts. "Back in the summer of 1982, I was teaching tennis in Carmel at John Gardner's Tennis Ranch while on college break. It was a prestigious camp, and many patrons were Hollywood people, politicians and the like. On days off, me and a buddy (who was also teaching at the Ranch) were ticking off the great courses of the Monterey peninsula. We decided that if we could get on Cypress, it would be the big enchilada. We mentioned to our boss (Jeff Stewart) that we'd love to get on Cypress. It turned out that he knew someone who knew someone who was a member. A few phone calls were made. On August 20th—two days before we had to leave Carmel and return to school—our boss told us that we'd play later that day. Our contact would come pick us up at 5 P.M. We'd have three hours and ten minutes of sunlight to get around. Word spread quickly around the ranch; we were getting requests from millionaire's kids to buy Cypress hats and shirts. Five o'clock came and went—our contact never showed. It was one of the great letdowns of my young life. We couldn't believe this had happened.

"Jeff, who was usually deferential to friends of the ranch, was equally disappointed, and followed up on our behalf. The next thing we knew, we had a tee time the following day at 11:30, and Jeff had given us the day off to go and play. Needless to say, Cypress Point lived up to all of my preconceived notions. It was a spectacular sunny day, just the right amount of breeze. For much of the round, I believe we were the only two people on the course. The caddie who was assigned to us had been there for thirty-five years, and had carried for players who had notched two of the five aces that have been logged on the 16th hole since 1928. I took this as good karma."

The 15th and 16th holes at Cypress Point are without a doubt the world's most famous back-to-back par 3s. While architecture aficionados are inclined to pontificate on the infinite values of the 16th, it was the 15th that had captured Joe's imagination before he ever stepped onto the course. There was no letdown when he actually got to play it. "I have always been relatively short and straight on the course, and felt that the 15th at Cypress was a hole I was born to play. After all, it's just 143 yards from the tips, 130 yards from the whites. After the 14th hole, you crawl out of a forest reverie where deer might be munching ice plants, cross 17 Mile Drive, then duck through some overhanging limbs and

OPPOSITE:
Two of golf's
most famous
par 3s—the 15th
and 16th at
Cypress Point.

shrubbery on a little dirt path . . . and emerge to a vista that's so beautiful you struggle for words—the green with its elegantly carved bunkers, the ocean crashing, the 16th hole in the distance. It's not only my favorite golf hole—it may be my most favorite place to be on the earth. On top of this, you get the golf shot—the shot I'd been waiting for all my life. That time, I dumped my 8-iron into a bunker, blasted out weakly and two-putted for four. My buddy, of course, hit the green, which I deeply resented at the time.

"Twenty-two years later, on my second round at Cypress Point, I hit the green and two-putted for par."

JOE PASSOV is architecture and course rankings editor for *Golf* magazine. He has written more than 750 articles for nearly sixty publications since 1987. He is also the author of *The Unofficial Guide to Golf Vacations in the Eastern U.S.* He has been a staff editor at four golf publications and was formerly editor in chief of *LINKS* magazine. He has played more than 1,200 courses in forty-six states and twenty-one countries.

If You Go

▶ **Getting There:** Cypress Point and the other attractions of greater Carmel are within a few hours' drive from the San Jose and San Francisco airports.

▶ **Course Information:** Par 72 Cypress Point plays 6,536 yards, with a slope rating of 136. It is not easy to finagle an invitation to Cypress Point; if the opportunity ever comes your way, by all means go! Guest green fees are $175.

▶ **Accommodations:** The many lodging options available around greater Monterey are highlighted at the Chambers of Commerce of Carmel (800-550-4333; www.carmelcalifornia.org), Pacific Grove (800-656-6650; www.pacificgrove.org), and Monterey (831-648-5360; www.mpcc.com); prices will tend to decrease as you move north.

HARDING PARK

RECOMMENDED BY **Frank D. "Sandy" Tatum Jr.**

In 1937, Harding Park, a cypress-dotted municipal golf course resting upon Lake Merced in the southwest corner of San Francisco, hosted its first U.S. Public Links Championship. By the 1960s, the course had become a regular stop on the PGA Tour.

In 1998, Harding Park was used as a parking lot for spectators attending the U.S. Open at the nearby Olympic Club. It was shortly thereafter that former USGA president and long-time Harding patron Sandy Tatum took it upon himself to build the coalitions that would be necessary to restore Harding to its former glory.

"I played in the San Francisco City Championship for thirty years beginning in the late thirties, which at that time were held at Harding Park," Sandy recalled. "It was a marvelous amateur competition with a great mix of people—you might find yourself pitted against a CEO or a plumber. Greats like Ken Venturi and Harvey Ward also competed. In the setting of the City Championship, I played Harding enough to get a sense of its quality and attractiveness. I don't recall exactly what brought me there in the late nineties, but I do remember that looking at the place, I was horrified. The course was turning into a weed patch; beyond the grand cypress trees and the lake, it had lost everything. I thought it was at risk of deteriorating beyond the point of people being able to play on it, and I wanted to help make sure that such a disaster was avoided.

"In my golfing life, I've been able to play every great golf course I could hope to play—Cypress Point, San Francisco Golf Club, Pine Valley," Sandy added. "I'm acutely aware of the added dimensions a player gets from playing a first-rate course in first-rate condition. This used to be the case at many municipal courses, but in the post–World War II era, most munis have deteriorated to be second- and third-rate courses. I think that we should have as many as possible that provide the public with a first-rate golf experience."

Harding Park was designed by Scotsman Willie Watson and opened for play in 1925. (Watson, who also designed the initial incarnation of the Lake Course at the adjacent Olympic Club, was compensated $300 for his efforts at Harding.) The gently rolling site is marked by an abundance of mature Monterey cypress; a ball struck into a copse of cypress will likely be found, though the trees are thick enough that you'll find yourself chipping back to the fairway before proceeding to the green. Players visiting in the early morning or later afternoon are likely to find themselves swathed in San Francisco's famous fog, which lends the tree-lined fairways a mysterious, monochromatic beauty. In Watson's original routing, the first nine sits in the center of the site, and the second nine circles around the perimeter, coming along the lake on the last few holes. This routing has been preserved in Harding's revitalized incarnation. "The aesthetics build dramatically as you come to the last five holes," Sandy continued. "The earlier holes set the scene nicely." (If the fog isn't too thick, you can spy the property of the venerable Olympic Club across Lake Merced from four of the last five holes.)

The story of how Harding Park came to be resuscitated is the stuff of graduate seminars in public policy or business administration. Sandy Tatum, who's had a successful legal career as well as a storied golfing life, quickly sized up the situation. "In my mind, there was no question that the course could be effectively renovated, but I knew that it would cost a great deal of money. I knew the city of San Francisco didn't have that kind of money. My hope was that we could lure a tour event to Harding, which would give the course an identity that could sustain a green fee structure that's affordable for San Francisco residents and priced for nonresidents to be able to finance the whole project." Sandy was eventually able to lure PGA commissioner Tim Finchem out to San Francisco, and the timing was right, as the PGA was looking for a West Coast venue for an event. Finchem dispatched Chris Gray, director of design for PGA Tour Design Services, to Harding, and he saw the course's potential as a tour venue. Meanwhile, the city commissioned research to spell out the economic benefits that future PGA events—and a world-class public golf course—would provide for San Francisco. There were more than a few bumps along the road, but the deal was eventually signed. And on October 9th, 2005, Tiger Woods won the first professional tourney to be staged at Harding in nearly forty years—the World Golf Championship–American Express—in a sudden-death playoff against John Daly. As of this writing, five more professional golf events are slated for Harding over the next fifteen years.

OPPOSITE:

The final five holes at Harding (including the short par 4 17th) follow the Lake Merced shoreline.

It's uncertain whether the Olympic Club will extend use of their facility for overflow parking.

Though the routing of Harding remains essentially the same as it was in Willie Watson's day, three fundamental changes were made to make the course tournament ready. "First, the tee for the fourth hole had to be moved back to both diminish the dogleg and stretch the hole into a par 5," Sandy described. "Second, we felt that moving the 13th green would turn a reasonably good par 4 into an excellent par 4. Finally, we wanted to stretch out the 18th. This required relocating the green to the former site of a practice green that was by the old clubhouse [also relocated], and commandeering what was once a section of the course's parking lot for the back tee." The 18th is indeed a striking finisher, a 440-yard par 4 (longer for professional events) that curves gently uphill. Your tee shot must cross over a generous portion of the northern section of Lake Merced; if you play over more of the lake, you can shorten your approach; if you opt for a safer play, beware of the bunkers on the right. There's no rest after your tee shot and what will be a fairly long (for most players) mid- to long-iron approach. Eighteen's multilevel green, which slopes precipitously back toward the fairway, yields more than its share of three-putts.

"Some courses have what I call an emotional feature," Sandy ventured. "They engage you as a golfer, but also on a deeper level. I have that feeling about Harding. One night, about a month after the renovated course had opened, I was walking toward my car, the last car in the parking lot. A young African-American man approached me and asked if I was Sandy Tatum. When I said yes, he said, 'I want to tell you how much this course means to me.' Both of us almost broke into tears."

FRANK D. "SANDY" TATUM JR. is a retired partner of the law firm of Cooley Godward Kronish, though he continues to practice general commercial law, having done so since 1950. He is a past president of the USGA and was closely involved with the design and development of golf courses in conjunction with real-estate development projects, including The Links at Spanish Bay. Frank has been a member of the San Francisco Mayor's Fiscal Advisory Committee and a trustee of Stanford University. In addition, he has been a member of the boards of directors of several organizations, including the Legal Aid Society (serving as president); Youth Law Center; United Bay Area Crusade; St. Elizabeth's Infant Hospital of San Francisco (chairman of the Finance Committee); and the San Francisco Mental Health Association.

If You Go

▶ **Getting There:** Harding Park is in the southwest corner of San Francisco, a $30 cab ride from either downtown or the San Francisco International Airport. If you happen to visit while they're playing a major at the Olympic Club, just head toward the roars of the cheering crowds.

▶ **Course Information:** Harding Park (415-664-4690; www.harding-park.com) plays to a par 72, and is 6,845 yards from the blue tees, with a slope rating of 126. Green fees are $155.

▶ **Accommodations:** No other city of its size can offer the abundance of eclectic accommodations, fine eateries, and classic watering holes that San Francisco serves up. A good place to start your planning is the San Francisco Convention and Visitors Bureau (415-974-6900; www.sfvisitor.org). While the trendy restaurants are ever-changing, the best bars have staying power. The Redwood Room (in the Clift Hotel, near Union Square) and Vesuvios (on Columbus in North Beach) are as different as could be, and both wonderful.

SPRING CITY GOLF AND LAKE RESORT

RECOMMENDED BY **Gordon Dalgleish**

9

DESTINATION

As its performance in the 2008 Summer Olympics vividly displayed, China has invested heavily in its sports infrastructure. Gymnastics, ping pong, and diving have benefited from an estimated annual investment of 800 million yuan ($117 million) in Olympic sports by the state (plus a nearly equal amount raised by state-run lotteries). The government's sporting zeal has not extended to golf—at least not *officially*. As Shanghai-based writer Dan Washburn has pointed out on ESPN.com, golf is

> . . . an activity loaded with political implications; there's a reason why the sport, which earned the nickname "green opium," was nowhere to be found during the first thirty-five years of the Communist regime. Golf, the belief goes, is an aristocratic, individualistic, even capitalistic pursuit, linked to corruption in the minds of many. And in today's China, although it is slowly becoming more accessible, golf indeed remains a rich man's game.

While there were no golf courses in China before 1984, it's estimated that the nation will have nearly 500 by 2010. Big-name architects from America and Europe have flocked to China, both to make the most of the opportunities (1.3 billion potential golfers!) and to make their mark on a heretofore blank canvas. Golf—and perhaps more significantly, golf course maintenance—is still a new concept for Chinese golf entrepreneurs, and many courses may fall a bit short of North American expectations. For Gordon Dalgleish, whose company leads golf-oriented tours to China, one set of courses that doesn't disappoint is found at Spring City. "The tracks here—the Mountain Course (designed by Jack Nicklaus) and the Lake Course (designed by Robert Trent Jones, Jr.)—are well designed, challenging by international standards, and among the most consistently well manicured in the country," Gordon said. "If these courses were in Kansas, they'd be recognized as good, if not miraculous. In China, a good course by Western standards becomes a *really good* golf course."

Spring City Golf and Lake Resort is situated in the province of Yunnan in southern China, which borders Myanmar, Laos, and Vietnam. It's just outside the provincial capital of Kunming, a three-hour plane ride from Beijing, on the shores of Yang Zong Hai Lake; the courses rest at nearly 7,000 feet. In many ways, Spring City is representative of many higher-end U.S. golf resort complexes; its promotional description, "A premier integrated golf resort comprising luxury villas and two championship golf courses," could've been lifted from a brochure for a property outside Scottsdale or Hilton Head. "Of the courses I've visited in China, the Spring City properties most closely resemble a Western facility in terms of operations," Gordon continued. "Both courses have lovely views of the surrounding mountains and the lake. Though both are first-rate, I particularly like some of the waterside holes on the Lake course, namely 7, 8, and 9." The 7th is a moderate par 4 (388 yards) where aggressive drivers can opt to play over a deep canyon on the most direct route to the green; if the winds are up or you lack nerve, there's a generous landing area on the left. If you miss the smallish green to the right, a sharp decline of twenty feet makes for a perilous pitch back. The dramatic par 3 8th hole plays 172 yards out and nearly 100 feet down from an elevated tee to the lakeshore. The par 5 9th plays along the lake, and is quite reachable for bigger hitters, though shots that drift to the right will find water.

Gordon Dalgleish had one of his more amusing cultural experiences at Spring City, while trying to play the 7th, 8th, and 9th holes at the Lake course. "I was doing a whirlwind tour of China's golf courses with a few journalists, including Joe Passov," Gordon recalled, "and we had a day at Spring City. We were supposed to play the Mountain and Lake courses and then head to Brilliant Spa and a cultural show, and we were tight for time. After playing the Mountain course, we teed off on the 10th at the Lake. Joe had heard about the last three holes on the front—the course's signature stretch—and after we played the back, he wanted to see those three holes. Our Chinese hosts couldn't comprehend why we would want to play just 7, 8, and 9 when we could play the whole nine. It's remarkably simple when you and I speak about it in English, but for them it was utterly incomprehensible. It took nearly thirty minutes to explain and get them to acquiesce—about as long as it would have taken to play the holes. I felt like Kofi Annan negotiating a difficult ceasefire."

As the above tale illustrates, a golfing journey to China cannot help but be a cultural journey as well. After a round at Spring City, Gordon was treated to another cultural exchange—this time with some fish. "Ten minutes from the Spring City Complex, there's an establishment called the Brilliant Spa," he recounted. "It's an immense facility, something like 400,000 square feet, with twenty-six different hot pools and every spa service you can imagine. The short drive to Brilliant Spa is jarring, as you go from the Western-style Spring City, through an extremely rural (and by some standards undeveloped) village, to this opulent structure. Our hosts insisted that we join them for a soak in the thermal pools. In one, there were small fish that would gently nibble on your feet and legs, eating any dry skin. I'm not a big spa person, but I was in awe."

GORDON DALGLEISH is a founding director of Perry Golf, a leading provider of golf travel to Scotland, England and Wales, Ireland, France, Spain and Portugal, Italy, South Africa, Australia, New Zealand, and China. A native Glaswegian, Gordon has served as a member of the board of directors of the American Junior Golf Association (1988–2000), and as a panelist for *Golf* magazine's Top 100 Courses. He's been recognized by *Condé Nast Traveler* magazine as one of the top travel specialists in the United States.

If You Go

▶ **Getting There:** Spring City Golf and Lake Resort (www.springcityresort.com) is an hour outside the city of Kunming, which is served by several airlines, including Air China (800-882-8122; www.airchina.com) and Cathay Pacific (800-233-2742; www.cathaypacific.com).

▶ **Course Information:** The Lake Course plays 7,204 yards to a par 72; the Mountain Course plays 7,453 to a par 72. Green fees are $118 for hotel guests, $283 USD for non-guests. For tee times, call +86 871 7671188, Ext. 1122.

▶ **Accommodations:** Lodging is available at Spring City, and golf packages are available. Gordon Dalgleish's company, Perry Golf (800-344-5257; www.perrygolf.com) leads golf/cultural tours to China, coordinating all the details along the way.

JADE DRAGON

SNOW MOUNTAIN GOLF CLUB

RECOMMENDED BY **Jeff Wallach**

"Modern China is a land of superlatives," Jeff Wallach declared. "It seems that whatever is constructed—be it a building or a golf course—needs to have an adjective attached that ends in 'est'—biggest, longest, hardest." That's at least one explanation for a golf course that stretches 8,548 yards, Jade Dragon Snow Mountain—as of this writing the world's longest golf course. "One can only hope that no one feels compelled to build a course that's any longer," Jeff added. "And God help anyone who is manic enough to play the thing from the back tees!"

The 2008 British Open at Royal Birkdale illustrated that a course needn't be back-breakingly long (nor peppered with water hazards!) to be difficult; Padraig Harrington's winning score on the seemingly modest par 70 7,173-yard layout was a 3+ 283. Yet through the middle and late twentieth century, courses kept growing. Some say it was to accommodate advances in equipment; others, that it was to give bragging rights to certain architects, and to fuel the egos of those players with enough machismo to step to the back tee . . . though in the latter case, most have no good reason beyond unchecked ego to be playing from the tips! The 8,000-yard barrier was first broken in 1964 at Dub's Dread Golf Club in Kansas City, which measured in at 8,204 yards (it's since been cut back by over 1,000 yards). In 1972, the Pines Course at the International Golf Club in Bolton, Massachusetts, was remodeled by Robert Trent Jones, Sr., to become the world's longest course, measuring 8,325 yards from "The Tiger" tees (this, of course, before the birth of Mr. Woods); at least the par from there is 77. (Australia has gone the International and even Jade Dragon one step better; a series of holes is being construct-ed across the Nullarbor Plain, a treeless desert stretching from the town of Kalgoorlie in West Australia to Ceduna in the south. The eighteen-hole track—which is taking

shape to spur tourism in this rather inhospitable and infrequently visited region—will stretch some 750 miles.)

Jade Dragon Snow Mountain Golf Club is located north of the city of Lijiang, in the northwestern corner of the Yunnan province. It takes its name from an immense glacier—twenty-two miles long and thirteen miles wide—that a long-ago observer looking north from Lijiang decided resembled a green dragon reclining in the clouds. The course rests near the base of the glacier—which is to say at a height of 10,000 feet. "When Jade Dragon's length comes up in conversation, people are always quick to point out that given the altitude, the ball goes twenty percent farther," Jeff continued. "This is certainly true. But what people don't consider is that bad shots also go twenty percent further astray."

Given Jade Dragon Snow Mountain Golf Club's location, its altitude, and its length, the act of playing a round here has the aura of embarking on an expedition—as soon as you leave your hotel. "It's an epic drive from Lijiang to the course," Jeff described. "I visited with a group of other journalists, and as our hosts headed deeper and deeper into the mountains, it felt as though we were driving to another century. As we pushed further and further away from the civilization of Lijiang, I couldn't help but think, 'Okay, this is where they're going to pull over and kill us.' Eventually, you come into a clearing, and there's a clubhouse. When you step out of the car, you realize that you've entered a different season. I was wearing shorts and a golf shirt when we left Lijiang; I found myself reaching into my bag and putting on every article of clothing I had at my disposal. You'd wear an old scorecard if that's all you had.

"Inside the clubhouse, there's a large fireplace with a blazing fire. You're assigned your caddies—young women, as at many courses in Asia—who haven't quite mastered English, but know enough golf terms to get you around the course. Eventually you're ushered away from the fire toward the first tee. I had a small sense of foreboding, as if the fire might be my last comfort before beginning an adventure I might not return from. The first hole is a par 5, 681 yards from the back—a diminutive 606 yards from the blues, where my group played. There are a few forced carries over lakes, and you have to be careful to land your first carry short of the second lake—something of a mathematical feat, considering that you're not completely adjusted to the added distance you get from the 10,000-foot elevation." After the 600-plus-yard opener, things settle down a bit. There's a reasonable 517-yard par 4 on the 2nd hole, a chip shot 236-yard par 3 3rd—and then, on the 5th, a 711-yard par 5. "The course is meticulously maintained,

OPPOSITE:

If the mist in the distance clears away, you'll be treated to vistas of Himalayan peaks surpassing 18,000 feet.

10

DESTINATION

53

especially given the alpine setting," Jeff added. "And we had the course nearly to our-selves—not because it's expensive, but because you might have an easier time reaching the polar ice caps. But after walking off the 503-yard 9th (just 462 yards from the blues), I did have a moment when I wondered if I could sneak back to the clubhouse and the hearth without anyone noticing."

It was an overcast day when Jeff played Jade Dragon Snow Mountain, and a certain lack of oxygen and the need for many layers of clothing made the altitude apparent. ("You felt at times like you were under water," Jeff added. "I'm fairly certain there were atten-dants with oxygen tanks riding around the course.") But the drama of the setting really hit home when the clouds began to lift. "I remember being up on an elevated tee as the sky began to clear. We thought the hills we'd seen around the course were mountains—then the real mountains were revealed, so enormously high that it was almost beyond belief. The more the sky cleared, the larger the mountains that were slowly exposed." Shanzidou, the tallest of Jade Dragon Snow Mountain's thirteen peaks, reaches 18,360 feet; these are the Himalayas, after all!

The course ends with a 695-yard par 5, and then the fireplace beckons. "If you have the energy left to tee the ball up on the 18th, you're winning," Jeff quipped. "But there are rewards waiting in the clubhouse after your epic day. They have a Japanese-style soaking tub and a restaurant that serves terrific food. But best of all, you have a real sense of accomplishment, like you've swum the English Channel or climbed a mountain (which you kind of have). Given the grandeur of the setting and the altitude and the course's absurd length, it's safe to assume that no one will ever build such a course again. And you've conquered it."

JEFF WALLACH is the award-winning author of five books, including *Beyond the Fairway* and *What the River Says*. He has also published more than 600 articles, essays, and fea-tures in such magazines as *Sports Illustrated, Men's Health, Men's Journal, Golf, Golf Digest, Travel & Leisure Golf, Continental Airlines,* and many others. Jeff believes he is the only writer to ever sell the same story to *Popular Science* and *Seventeen* magazines. He is also cofounder of The Critical Faculty, a golf/travel consulting firm, and has done branding and marketing for many clients in the golf and travel industries. Jeff lives with his wife in Portland, Oregon, where he golfs, bikes, plays squash and soccer, and takes a lot of ibu-profen. He claims to have a pretty good short game for a journalist.

If You Go

► **Getting There:** Jade Dragon Snow Mountain Golf Club (+86 888 513 1888) is near the city of Lijiang, which can be reached via domestic flights from Kunming, Shanghai, and Beijing. Several domestic airlines serve the city, including Air China (800-882-8122; www.airchina.com) and China Eastern Airlines (www.ce-air.com).

► **Course Information:** Jade Dragon plays 8,548 yards (yes, that's two eights) to a par 72. Green fees range from $70 to $117.

► **Accommodations:** Banyan Tree Lijiang (800-591-0439; www.banyantree.com/lijiang/index.html) is a luxurious option in greater Lijiang. A more modest but still quite acceptable option is the Lijiang International Hotel (+86 888 588 8888).

DESTINATION

10

MERSEYSIDE

RECOMMENDED BY **Bob Wood**

"I love golf, but I also really enjoy English football [soccer]," Bob Wood began. "Merseyside is home to some of England's most outstanding golf courses, plus six premier-league football teams. If you go over during the season [August through May], you can combine a fine game of golf with first-rate football spectating, even in the same day."

The county of Merseyside, in northwest England, officially incorporates the boroughs of Birkenhead, Wallasey, Liverpool, Bootle, and St. Helens, radiating north and south from the banks of the Mersey River. From a golf visitor perspective, Merseyside can be said to extend north up the coast to Southport and Lytham St. Anne's; from a footballer's perspective, it reaches east to Manchester. Tourism interests have dubbed the stretch from Blackpool in the north to Wirral in the south "England's Golf Coast," and with good reason—there are twenty courses within an hour (give or take) of Southport, including three venues on the current British Open rota: Royal Birkdale, Royal Lytham St. Anne's, and Royal Liverpool. Within fifteen minutes of the seaside resort town (which has been likened to an English version of Carmel, California), there are five other golf links that could easily host an Open. These include Hillside and Southport and Ainsdale.

The Hillside Golf Club was established in 1911 as a nine-hole layout. Its first big change came in 1923 when the course was relocated to its current locale, literally a short-iron from Royal Birkdale, in the Birkdale Hills. The second big change occurred in 1967, when the redesigned course (featuring a new back nine) opened for play. Many who have played both courses feel that Hillside is every bit the layout of its revered neighbor. "The back nine is built into and around a series of huge dunes," Bob described. "The front is pleasant, if unremarkable, but the back is easily one of the most spectacular nines I've ever seen. The contrast is considerable." One peak at Hillside is reached at the 11th hole,

OPPOSITE:
Southport and Ainsdale is not on the Open Rota, though it's every bit the challenge of nearby Royal Birkdale.

a 508-yard par 5. The tee rests atop a sand dune; once you've made the climb, you're rewarded with a panoramic view of the Irish Sea, and a number of golf holes—both on Hillside, and at neighboring Royal Birkdale and Southport and Ainsdale. "I played Hillside during the week of the British Open," Bob continued. "From the 11th, you can look right at the 18th hole, with the grandstands and TV towers. I've attended a number of British Opens, but this gave me a very different perspective—seeing the venue from another world-class course."

Like Hillside, Southport and Ainsdale started its life as a nine-hole course, in 1906. Not long after, the club was relocated to its current location across the train line from Hillside, and expanded to eighteen holes. In 1923, the new course received a facelift from Scotsman James Braid, a gifted player (and contemporary of Harry Varden) who won five British Opens. Braid was nearly as gifted on the boards as he was on the fairways, designing or remodeling more than 200 courses around the United Kingdom, including redesigns at Carnoustie, Troon, and Prestwick. At S&A (as the club is affectionately known), he built six new holes and reworked twelve others among the sandhills, heather, and gorse; fifteen of the original eighteen holes exist today, much as Braid intended. S&A has been called one of the finest links designs in England. "Southport and Ainsdale is an authentic links layout, though it's not directly on the ocean," Bob said. "It has a very natural flow, and the members there are quite friendly. It made some of its reputation as the first course to host the Ryder Cup twice, in 1933 and 1937." The hole most likely to stay with you once you've left S&A is the par 5 16th, dubbed "Gumbleys" (named for one of the club's founding members). You'll aim your drive at a large bunker some 300 yards out, lined above with a bank of "sleepers" (English parlance for railroad ties). From here, it's a blind approach to a long, narrow green, backed by a sprawling dune.

The appeal of a visit to Merseyside goes beyond its fabulous coastal courses. Manchester and Liverpool are thriving cities, a perfect counterpoint to the charming resort town of Southport. (What Beatles fan could resist the chance to tour the boyhood homes of John and Paul, or to board a "Magical Mystery Tour" bus to see Penny Lane and Strawberry Fields in Liverpool?) The Lake District, which inspired poets of an earlier age, is also an easy drive away and showcases England's most beautiful mountain scenery.

And there's the football.

In 2008, Bob had the chance to travel to Merseyside on several occasions, thanks in part to the hosting of the British Open at Royal Birkdale. "My first visit was in May," Bob recalled, "and one Sunday we drove out to Southport from Liverpool in the morning and played Birkdale. We had the kind of weather that the players experienced during the Open—which is to say, five different kinds of weather! We spoke to some members about the changes that had been made to the course in preparation for the tournament. One of the most significant modifications was made to the 17th green. When we got there, it was out of character relative to the other greens on the course—knobby and multi-tiered. There were only four or five spots where the pin could be placed. It turned out to be an important hole during the Open—Padraig Harrington made an eagle here on the final day to seal his victory, while second place finisher Ian Poulter took three putts here on Sunday. After our round, we headed back to Liverpool and Anfield Stadium to see the Liverpool football club play Manchester City. Liverpool is one of the best-known clubs in the Premier League and Anfield is one of the most famous stadiums. It was the ultimate day."

BOB WOOD is a twenty-eight-year veteran of Nike, where he served as president of Nike Golf from 1998 to 2008. He was born and raised in Southern California and majored in viticulture at the University of California, Davis. His career at Nike includes time as vice president for footwear product marketing and vice president for U.S. marketing. His passions include his family, playing electric and acoustic guitar, skiing, golf, and, of course, football. He supports Arsenal Football Club, based in London.

If You Go

▶ **Getting There:** England's Golf Coast is most easily reached from Manchester, which has nonstop service from New York on several airlines, including Continental (800-231-0856; www.continental.com).

▶ **Course Information:** Hillside (+44 1704 567169; www.hillside-golfclub.co.uk) plays 6,850 yards from the back tees to a par 72. Green fees range from £75 to £95. Southport and Ainsdale (+44 1704 578000; www.sandagolfclub.co.uk) plays 6,768 yards to a par 72. Green fees range from £65 to £90.

▶ **Accommodations:** The England's Golf Coast website (www.englandsgolfcoast.com) lists accommodations around Southport and beyond.

ROYAL NORTH DEVON

RECOMMENDED BY **Ran Morrissett**

The Old Course at St. Andrews is called "the home of golf." Royal North Devon (known simply as "Westward Ho!" in some circles, and as "RND" by members) has been called "the St. Andrews of England." One source for the sobriquet is the fact that Royal North Devon is the oldest extant golf course in England, dating back to 1864. Beyond its long history in County Devon, Westward Ho! bears other similarities to the Old Course. "It doesn't look much like a golf course at first glance," Ran Morrissett began, "in that it's not an obviously manmade environment. To me, that's the point—golf should reconnect the player with nature. The American version of golf in many instances is a hollower version of the game that you see at a place like Westward Ho! Essentially, there's no substance in the experience of riding in a golf cart for five hours between rows of condominiums. This doesn't lift your spirits or help you bond with your family or forget your worries at work. Westward Ho! connects you back with the natural world. There are super-wide vistas, and you're very conscious of the expansiveness of the property, and your spirit soars!"

Westward Ho! is a small village on the Bristol Channel, in the far southwestern corner of England. (The exclamation point is part of the town's name, which is derived from the title of a novel by Charles Kingsley.) The original course here was staked out by the ever-industrious Old Tom Morris, though few elements of his layout remain. (One hardy exception is the immense bunker on the 355-yard par 4 4th hole, which is reinforced by fifteen-foot planking; though it's but 170 yards from the tee, flying a drive over this edifice is an exhilarating moment.) Englishman W. H. Fowler deserves the credit for the course that golfers enjoy today. Fowler was a major figure in the "golden age of golf course architecture," designing such British notables as Walton Heath and Cruden Bay, and Eastward Ho! on Cape Cod in the United States. He's also credited with transforming the 18th at

60

Pebble Beach into a par 5, in 1922. "The hand of man is very light on Fowler's courses," Ran continued. "In fact, it's so light that there are no trademark elements, meaning you can't obviously identify one of his courses as his design. It's so different today. Designers are compelled to make their mark, in part to justify their 'name brand' fee. This notion just didn't exist at the turn of the last century."

If vertigo-inducing dunes are an essential element in your picture of perfect links land, Westward Ho! may not initially capture your interest. "Westward Ho! seems very flat, but I think that we often forget that a two- to four-foot roll is all you need to lend a course the nuances that make for great-quality golf," Ran opined. "Just because you have 100-foot-tall dunes in all directions doesn't mean you'll be able to build a great course. Westward Ho! has countless little bumps and hollows. It's laid across common ground, which means that farmers can graze their animals here. The greens are circled with white string eight to ten inches off the ground so local cattle and sheep don't trample the putting surfaces. When you stand on some of the tees—say the 3rd—it's not well defined how you're supposed to play the course. If you stand on a parkland course, you have a linear path to the hole marked out by a tree line or the cut of a fairway. You don't have that at Westward Ho!—nature doesn't embrace linearity." Some of the holes play across pasture land, some along the ridge that separates the course from the ocean, and others through a veritable sea of rushes. The variety of its hazards, along with its constantly changing terrain and glorious setting, explain Westward Ho!'s appeal.

If there's one hole that defines Westward Ho! for Ran, it's the 406-yard par 4 6th. "As far as I'm concerned, the elevated tee on the 6th is the most glorious spot in all of English golf," Ran effused. "You can look across Pegwell Bay for twenty miles, hear the surf pounding off to the left, feel the wind blowing in off the ocean. The fairway down below is humpy-bumpy—mercifully, no bulldozer ever got near the property. If this were a modern $10 million construction, the dozers would have obliterated all those humps and bumps. All these nuances shine through, and they make the hole play differently every single time. On one occasion you'll be on the downward side of a hump, next time you'll be on the upward side. You're always having to tweak your stance and your swing, depending on your lie and the wind. From my perspective, you just can't beat it. I'm so taken with the hole that I commissioned a huge painting from an artist named Mike Miller depicting the 6th as viewed from the tee. It hangs in my living room, so you can't miss it when you walk in the house."

Past connoisseurs of the game of golf have written lovingly of Westward Ho!, including chroniclers like Bernard Darwin and Pat Ward-Thomas. Indeed, in a 1939 compendium of the world's top 100 courses, assembled by a short-lived publication called *The National Golf Review*, Westward Ho! was ranked sixteenth in the world. "I serve on *Golf Digest*'s Top 100 courses panel, and it saddens me that a course like Westward Ho! has little chance of making the list today," Ran observed. "Nothing has changed at the course in the last forty years, or the last eighty, for that matter. The perception of what makes a great golf course has changed. First, there's the false fascination with conditioning as represented by Augusta National and other such over-manicured courses. Thanks in part to the animals (mentioned above) and modest greenskeeping budgets, you will not find 'perfect' conditioning at Westward Ho!. Second, the course may not jibe with some people's notion of fairness. For some, to split the 6th fairway and ask players to hit a utility wood from a sloping lie off a hummock to an uphill green would be considered unfair. For the rest of us who place the most importance on variety and challenging fun in an inspired setting, then Westward Ho! remains one of the half dozen most engaging links to visit and get to know."

RAN MORRISSETT is founder and editor of Golf Club Atlas (www.golfclubatlas.com), a noncommercial website devoted to frank commentary on golf course architecture.

If You Go

▶ **Getting There:** Westward Ho! is in County Devon, best reached from Bristol, which is served by many carriers, including Continental Airlines (800-231-0856; www.continental. com).

▶ **Course Information:** Westward Ho! (+44 1237 477598; www.royalnorthdevongolf-club.co.uk) measures 6,653 yards from the white (in England, back) tees, and plays to a par 72. Green fees run from £40 to £46.

▶ **Accommodations:** A list of local lodging options is available on the Westward Ho! website, www.royalnorthdevongolfclub.co.uk/localaccommodation.html.

SPERONE GOLF CLUB

RECOMMENDED BY **Christopher Smith**

It would be an understatement to say that Napoleone di Buonaparte (who later changed his name to Napoleon Bonaparte to de-emphasize his Tuscan heritage) had aggressive inclinations. One can only wonder if some of his hostile tendencies might have been softened by an early introduction to golf in his native Corsica. He might have come to appreciate the calming effects of a closer interaction with nature. He might have learned to rein in any frustrations stemming from perceived inadequacies (not long off the tee?) and channel them toward new self-improvements (spend time with the short game).

If only Sperone Golf Club had been built 220 years earlier!

Sperone is situated near the town of Bonifacio, at the extreme southern end of the island of Corsica—which means at the extreme southern end of France. (Corsica's not only geographically isolated from the rest of France; through much of its modern history, it was aligned with Genoa [once a republic of Italy], which explains in part why Napoleone's family made its way here from Tuscany.) "Sperone has to be the most aesthetically pleasing course that I've ever seen," Christopher Smith said. "There are turquoise waters, rocky cliffs, and views of the hills of the island of Sardinia in the distance [Sardinia is less than seven miles away across the Strait of Bonifacio]. I have played courses with more intriguing designs, but no other course with such a phenomenal setting. The other great appeal of playing Sperone is Corsica itself. The first time I visited was nearly twenty years ago, right after the course opened. Twenty years later, the area looks the same, having retained its rustic qualities. The island is not extensively developed; citizens rely on low-key tourism and the cultivation of chestnuts and lemons to make a living. There's a charm to places like Corsica, places that seem stuck in a time warp, a sort of strange twilight zone. It will always bring me back."

Sperone Golf Club was designed by Robert Trent Jones, Sr., one of history's most prolific architects—certainly the most prolific, were you to add the creations of his progeny, Robert Trent, Jr. and Rees, to his list of course credits. (Jones, Sr. had his hand in some 500 designs—350 originals, 150 remodels; only Donald Ross is credited with more layouts, though Ross didn't often visit the sites where his designs were implemented.) Jones was known—and sometimes reviled—for his punitive designs. These included his reinterpretations of classic courses (such as Augusta National, Baltusrol, the Olympic Club, and Oak Hill) to make them more challenging for major tournaments, which earned him the moniker "The Open Doctor." "The shattering of par without a proper challenge is a fraud," he often said. "I make them play par." This philosophy explains the yawning bunkers and seemingly unflyable lakes that permeate many of his properties.

In other ways, Robert Trent Jones, Sr. set the tone for generations of course architects to come. He was an early road warrior, logging an estimated eight million miles in delivering his designs to forty-five states and thirty-five foreign countries; he was fond of saying that "The sun never sets on a Robert Trent Jones golf course." He was not shy about moving earth, digging the aforementioned lakes to get the fill he'd need. Jones also understood the importance of salesmanship and promotion, and was adept at cultivating friends in important places—friends who could green-light important projects, like Sperone. (Jones had significant assistance on Sperone from Cabell Robinson, it should be noted.)

By RTJ, Sr. standards, Sperone is a relatively short course, coming in at 6,678 yards from the tips. When the wind is blowing off the Straits of Bonifacio, however, the course plays much, much longer. Twelve of the holes are inland, winding through the thick *maquis* shrubland that's found on much of Corsica; the other six holes—11 through 16—cling to the coastline, and have earned Sperone the sobriquet "the Pebble Beach of Europe." The par 4 11th begins with a blind tee shot uphill. As you crest the rise, the hills of northern Sardinia spread out before you, framing your approach. The 12th is a modest 147-yard par 3 along the coast, where your tee shot must carry scrubland for most of the distance. On a windy day, this shot can easily demand a fairway wood. The 13th is a short par 4 that continues along the coast; it's drivable if the wind is cooperating. If you wish to weigh the pros and cons of hitting for the eagle, consider a stop at the crescent-shaped beach that spreads below the path between the 12th green and 13th tee. "If things aren't going very well for you on the course, the pristine water below makes it tempting to give

OPPOSITE:
The 16th at Sperone, one of the holes that gained this Corsican jewel its reputation as "the Pebble Beach of Europe."

13

DESTINATION

up golf and simply go for a swim," Christopher added. If you do drop into the Mediterranean, be sure to dry off and trek on, as the best is yet to come. The par 5 16th is a fitting finale to Sperone's six-hole seaside swing. The back tees are on a spit of land that extends into the Strait of Bonifacio. From here, you'll aim over the white cliffs that comprise the southernmost headlands of Corsica. If you successfully take a big bite off this 580-yard par 5 with your tee shot, you can consider crossing the strait a second time en route to the green—though it will take two near-perfect shots to get there.

CHRISTOPHER SMITH is the PGA Lead Teaching Professional at Pumpkin Ridge Golf Club outside Portland, Oregon. His teaching and coaching experiences as a professional instructor since 1988 have included stints in Florida, New England, and Western Europe; his list of students includes Tour players, professional athletes, CEOs, top-ranked juniors—and recreational hackers. A Master Instructor with the Jim McLean Golf Schools, Christopher has been nominated by *Golf* magazine as one of the top 100 instructors in America, was named 2004 Pacific Northwest Section PGA Teacher of the Year and 2003 Oregon Chapter PGA Teacher of the Year, and was selected in 2003 and 2005 by *Golf Digest* as one of the top instructors in Oregon. He is a Bill Bowerman Advisory Staff member with Nike Golf. Christopher is the speed golf world record holder, having shot five under par for eighteen holes in forty-four minutes, six seconds at the 2005 Chicago Speed Golf Classic. He is the author of *I've Got 99 Swing Thoughts but "Hit the Ball" Ain't One* (2007) and the creator of the CD *Better Golf*.

If You Go

▶ **Getting There:** Bonifacio is most easily reached from the airport at Figari, which is served by CCM (www.aircorsica.com) and Air France (www.airfrance.com) via Paris, Lyons, and other mainland France airports.

▶ **Course Information:** Sperone (+33 495 731 713; www.sperone.net) plays 6,704 yards from the tips to a par 72. Green fees range from €60 to €95.

▶ **Accommodations:** The upscale Sperone resort (+33 825 078 466; www.sperone.net) has apartments and villas for rent. Visit Corsica (+33 4 95 51 00 00; http://english.visitcorsica.com) has an extensive list of lodging options in Bonifacio.

DESTINATION 13

CHANTILLY AND FONTAINEBLEAU

RECOMMENDED BY **James Dodson**

Twenty-somethings who fantasize about Paris as a place where they can immerse themselves in a cloud of Gitanes smoke, cheap-red-wine–fueled literary discussions, and unbridled romance probably do not think much about the City of Light's potential for golf. For that matter, neither do golf travelers—though there's a good reason they should. "I'd wanted to look at France from a golf perspective for a long time," James Dodson began, "even though it's not a place where golfers traditionally went. The opportunity came up when I became golf editor for American Express *Departures* magazine. The piece I really wanted to do concerned golf around Paris, as I'd heard there were some very good courses nearby. I was able to take my fiancée (now wife), Wendy, along, and enjoyed some of the best golfing days—maybe best days, period—of my life."

For the golf course architecture aficionado visiting Paris, it is not the artistry of Matisse and Manet that captivates so much as the work of Englishman Tom Simpson, who coined the phrase "the Golden Age of Architecture" for the 1920s and 1930s, when he did some of his most memorable work. In a fraternity of eccentrics and larger-than-life personalities, Simpson stood out. A Cambridge-trained barrister and scion of a wealthy family, he was known to show up at the sites of new commissions in a chauffeur-driven Rolls Royce, a not-so-quiet way to let his well-heeled employers know that he wasn't some commoner to be trifled with. Here's how George Peper imagined Simpson's arrival: "From the back seat emerges what appears to be a fugitive from the Cannes Film Festival, sporting an embroidered cape, horn-rimmed sunglasses, a floppy beret, and an attitude." Simpson left his mark in Great Britain (Cruden Bay and Berkshire along with a renovation of Sunningdale), Belgium (Royal Antwerp), Ireland (a reworking of Ballybunion), New Zealand (New Zealand Golf Club), and, perhaps most notably, France.

Three of his greatest works are here—Morfontaine, Chantilly, and Fontainebleau—along with a number of other designs. Like his fellow golden-agers, Simpson championed the notion of strategic golf course design, where different approach options are presented to the player; more demanding options (successfully executed!) are rewarded with a better position on the fairway or on the green. "Most American golf architecture fans know Robert Trent Jones, Donald Ross, and perhaps Old Tom Morris," Jim continued. But they don't know Tom Simpson. This is reason alone to golf in France, as he's one of the greatest architects of all time."

The extremely private Morfontaine did not figure on Jim and Wendy's itinerary, but Chantilly and Fontainebleau did. The stop at the parkland Vineuil course at Chantilly (a second course was added in 1991 by the dean of modern-day British architects, Donald Steel) capped off a fabulous day, the kind, in Jim's words, "that inspires travel posters and Visa commercials"—and encapsulates all the attractions of French golf travel. "We commenced the day dewsweeping a beautiful John Jacobs parkland course in the town of Apremont in just shy of three hours. We then pushed on to the ancient stone village of Senlis where we lunched at a fabulous patisserie and hoofed through the medieval cathedral where Joan of Arc once rallied her troops. We then followed a tunnel of magnificent sycamores along the picturesque River Oise to the market town of Compiègne, where my father had been stationed in World War II, and where there is a famous steeplechase course, which happened to be running its final race when we serendipitously ambled up. On a lark, we plunked down twenty francs on the number 8 horse and watched it gallop from dead last to win, sending an unexpected windfall of 144 francs back at us through the betting window, which we promptly squandered in the farmer's market on truffle-flavored vinegar, fresh raspberries, three kinds of cheese, and two bottles of locally pressed cabernet.

"Soon after we arrived at Chantilly, presented 800 francs to a girl named Marie (who was doing her nails), and strolled out to the empty first tee of the Vineuil course, which was a little like paying fifty bucks apiece and being pointed to the opening hole of Merion or Winged Foot while members are away at Rich Persons' Camp. That's a great characteristic of golf in France—you can call up the most illustrious course (Morfontaine excepted) and say you'd like to play. You're not only welcome—they seem astonished when you call. As we walked to the tee, there was only the sound of our footsteps and the cuckoos in the surrounding forest. Simpson was very fond of bunkering, especially the kind of daunting

OPPOSITE:

The cross-
bunkering
typical of Tom
Simpson's designs
is evident on
the 3rd hole at
Fontainebleau.

cross-bunkering you encounter on the first hole at Vineuil." The round proceeded as the reddening Van Gogh sun set and the cuckoos called, shots clearing (and occasionally finding) those amazing Simpson bunkers. It ended with Jim and Wendy being escorted to a bistro in Chantilly with some men who befriended them in the clubhouse, where they feasted on a steak au poivre "the size of a Michelin tire" . . . and one of their escorts suggesting they play Fontainebleau.

"The sun was coming up as I passed the grand palace at Fontainebleau, where Napoleon bade his troops farewell en route to exile," Jim continued, "and a few kilometers later reached the ultra-private club of the same name, at the edge of Europe's largest forest. The clubhouse gate was locked, but a wild-eyed elderly caretaker let me in and waved me in the general direction of the clubhouse, an adorable green-and-white Tudor-style manor house. I walked to the elevated first tee and took in a rough and sandy terrain that was reminiscent of both Pinehurst and Pine Valley. Instead of cuckoos, I heard contented doves. A young red-haired woman suddenly bounded up the clubhouse steps behind me, smiling and pleasantly greeting me. Having identified me as an American, Cely—the clubhouse manager—offered to make me coffee. She had no clue about the club's visitation policy or fee structure, but suggested I 'go and play the golf' and settle up with club authorities afterward."

"Fontainebleau has all of the usual Simpson trademarks," Jim said, "bunkers that look as if they've been there since Napoleon said good-bye to the troops, challenging approach shot angles (especially the blind approach on the par 5 8th) and putting surfaces that must be respected to avoid catastrophe." Along the way, he picked up an eagle and a playing partner named Marcel who turned out to be one of France's leading screenwriters, and to possess extremely strong (and not terribly sympathetic) views on the fall of Frenchman Jean Van de Veldt in the 1999 British Open. Jim also recorded his first score of even par in almost ten years.

A day later, after ascending the second platform of the largest golf tee in the world (sometimes called the Eiffel Tower), Jim and Wendy became engaged.

Vive la France!

JAMES DODSON was an award-winning columnist for *Golf* magazine for almost twenty years and travel editor for *Departures* magazine for a decade. A former senior writer for the *Atlanta Journal and Constitution Sunday* magazine and *Yankee* magazine, he has won numerous national awards for his public-affairs and political writing, including the William Allen White Award for Public Affairs Journalism given by the University of Kansas. His non-golf work has appeared in *Gentlemen's Quarterly, The New York Times, Sports Illustrated, Travel and Leisure, Town and Country, Reader's Digest, Geo, Outside*, and numerous other national publications. His book *Final Rounds* has sold 300,000 copies worldwide, received the International Network of Golf's industry honors award for best golf book of 1996, and is being produced as a feature film; and *Faithful Travelers* has been produced as a television movie. Jim's book with Arnold Palmer, *A Golfer's Life: The Autobiography of Arnold Palmer*, was a *New York Times* bestseller. Among his other books are *The Dewsweepers, The Road to Somewhere: Travels with a Young Boy through an Old World, Ben Hogan: An American Life, Beautiful Madness: One Man's Journey through Other People's Gardens*, and *The Pinehurst Cure*.

If You Go

▶ **Getting There:** Chantilly and Fontainebleau are within an hour's drive of downtown Paris. Orly/Charles de Gaulle Airport is served by most major carriers, including Air France (www.airfrance.com).

▶ **Course Information:** Chantilly (+33 44 57 04 43: www.golfdechantilly.com) measures 6,396 yards from the back tees and plays to a par 71. Fontainebleau (+33 64 22 74 19; www.golfdefontainebleau.org) plays 6,643 yards from the tips to a par 72; it has a slope rating of 130. Though both clubs are private facilities, they're generally able to accommodate visiting golfers; the courtesy of a call a few days before your arrival will facilitate gaining access. Neither course publishes green fees.

▶ **Accommodations:** Whether you're seeking an apartment overlooking the Seine or a countryside chateau, The French Tourist Office (www.francetourism.com) can help.

DESTINATION 14

MAUNA KEA

RECOMMENDED BY **Darrin Gee**

There's a thrill that comes from visiting a new destination and finding that it defies every one of your expectations—but that it's still wonderful. There's also a thrill that comes from reaching that destination and finding that it perfectly matches the image you carried in your mind's eye. The latter is how Darrin Gee characterizes Mauna Kea. "For me, Mauna Kea frames the mainlander's vision of Hawaii golf in every conceivable way. There's a perfect juxtaposition of elevation changes, native vegetation, crystal-blue waters, expanses of lava, and emerald-green fairways. It's exactly what a Hawaii course should be. Mauna Kea is not only about aesthetics. It's a wonderful strategic design—holes that are challenging, but fair. There's also Mauna Kea's lore."

Mauna Kea lies near the northern tip of the island of Hawaii, on the Kohala Coast. It takes its name from a dormant volcano that looms to the south, a mountain that's tall enough (at 13,796 feet) to be frosted seasonally with a patina of snow, despite its tropical locale. (Mauna Kea translates from the Hawaiian language as "white mountain.") The original golf course at Mauna Kea and the adjoining Mauna Kea Beach Hotel (now operated by Prince Resorts Hawaii) was the vision of Laurance Rockefeller, the fourth son of John D. Rockefeller, Jr. Besides helping to oversee the family's investment and philanthropic interests, Rockefeller established resorts at several locales in the Caribbean. When he arrived in the early 1960s on the big island's Kohala Coast—then still largely undiscovered—he saw the potential for a world-class golf course amongst the vast expanses of black lava rock. He purchased nearly 2,000 acres above Hapuna Beach and Kauna'oa Bay and flew in the world's preeminent designer, Robert Trent Jones, Sr., to evaluate the possibilities. "The story goes," Darrin explained, "that after the two men walked the property, Rockefeller asked Jones if he could build a course. Jones picked up

OPPOSITE:
The famous 3rd at Mauna Kea, with its 200-plus-yard carry over the Pacific . . . at least from the back tees.

73

some lava, crushed it in his hands and replied, 'You will have your course.'" Thus, the fiftieth state's first great course was born. (Jones would later consider Mauna Kea among his three best original designs.)

"There are so many good holes at Mauna Kea," Darrin continued. "All four par 3s are great [each one plays over 200 yards from the back]. There are excellent short par 4s (including one that's potentially drivable), long par 5s that require two monster shots for a chance at eagle, and dogleg lefts and rights that require players to use lots of different shots." A great part of Mauna Kea's lore arose from its third hole, an audacious par 3 that in its original incarnation measured 261 yards from the tips—nearly all of that a two-and-a-half-football-fields carry over the Pacific, from one rocky promontory to the next. If the very existence of such a hole (with its green encircled by seven bunkers) weren't enough to put Mauna Kea on the golf map, a 1965 match orchestrated to help promote the new course would etch it onto the collective golf consciousness of a generation . . . and help begin to establish Hawaii as a golf destination. Arnold Palmer, Jack Nicklaus, and Gary Player—all in their prime—were invited to play a "skins"-style competition, the "Big Three Golf" series. Darrin picks up the story: "During the warm-up round, the three players went to the back tee on number 3, holding drivers. The wind is said to have been up that day, and only one of three was able to poke it to the green. Fearing embarrassment, one of the other players refused to play from the back tee on TV—and they instead played from the blues, which measure 210 yards over the water. For many years the back tee was closed for golfers and used instead for weddings. Now the back tee is open again. I have to say that whatever tee you choose, it's a spectacular shot; none of the drama is lost from the front tees." (Some sources identify Arnold Palmer as the long hitter on that fateful day in Mauna Kea's history; he would later return, with design partner Ed Seay, to design the sister course at Mauna Kea Beach Resort, Hapuna.)

It's worth noting that many players consider the 247-yard par 3 11th hole an even more challenging hole than number 3. It plays downhill 100 feet, which makes it a bit shorter than the card would imply. Four deep bunkers guard short right, short left, and short center, respectively; a shot that goes long is in the Pacific. Where number 3 is largely a play of strength—you make it or you don't—number 11 has a level of subtlety. A 3 here is well-earned; a 4 is nothing to be ashamed of.

Mauna Kea has just undergone a significant restoration. In a fitting passing of the torch, the work was led by Rees Jones, one of RTJ's golf-course-architect sons. "One major aspect of the restoration is the bunkering," Darrin explained. "They were deepened and fashioned to have higher lips. While the restoration work is welcome after forty-four years, it's a testament to Mauna Kea's quality that the course remains unchanged. If you happen to watch the broadcast of the Big Three match and then play the course, you'll see that it's the same, except that the trees are taller. It's withstood the test of time. To score, you have to think and play your best. To me, that's a sign of a classic course."

DARRIN GEE is golf's newest authority on the mental and inner aspects of the game. His Spirit of Golf Academy (www.spiritofgolfacademy.com), based at the Mauna Kea Resort and the Big Island Country Club, has been named one of the top golf schools in America by *Golf* magazine. Darrin's book *The Seven Principles of Golf* (STC, 2007) is considered a classic akin to Harvey Penick's *Little Red Book* and Ben Hogan's *Five Lessons*. His second book, *The Seven Personalities of Golf,* was published in 2008. He also released two top-selling mental game DVDs, *Mastering the Mental Game,* Volumes I and II. Darrin has been featured on radio, on TV, and in several bestselling golf instruction books, including *The Secret of Golf* by George Peper and *1,001 Reasons to Love Golf* (STC). He is a sought-after motivational speaker for corporations, incentives, meetings, and conventions throughout Hawaii, the U.S. mainland, and abroad.

If You Go

▶ **Getting There:** Mauna Kea is on the northern tip of the island of Hawaii, 26 miles from Kona. Kona is served by many major carriers, including Alaska Air (800-ALASKAAIR; www.alaskaair.com) and American Airlines (800-433-7300; www.aa.com).

▶ **Course Information:** Mauna Kea (800-882-6060; www.maunakeabeachhotel.com) plays 7,114 yards from the tips to a par 72, with a slope rating of 143. Green fees range from $125 to $175.

▶ **Accommodations:** There are two resorts on the premises at Mauna Kea—the Mauna Kea Beach Hotel and Hapuna Beach Hotel. Both are operated by Prince Resorts Hawaii (888-9PRINCE; http://princeresortshawaii.com).

PRINCEVILLE

RECOMMENDED BY **Amy Alcott**

When Hall of Famer Amy Alcott wants a respite from the pressures of professional golf, she sets her sights on Princeville. "I find that it's a spiritual paradise, and experience a great renewal being in that part of the world," Amy said. "The isolation of the north coast of Kauai and the beauty of the botanical gardens are both relaxing and rejuvenating. I first visited in the late seventies when I was coming back to the mainland from playing a junior golf event in Japan. Friends offered me the use of their condo and said I had to visit this special place. I've been going back ever since; for a time, I even had a home there, and represented Princeville on the tour. Princeville helped me during the biggest years of my career. It has nothing to do with golf and everything to do with golf at the same time."

Should you decide that you want to hit the ball around a bit while drinking in the natural wonders of Princeville, rumor has it that there are a few decent tracks nearby.

The Hawaiian island of Kauai is known as "The Garden Isle," thanks to the lushness of its volcanic hillsides, perennially cloaked in a riot of greens. The green is courtesy of the vast amounts of rain parts of Kauai receive; 5,148-foot Mt. Wai'ale'ale in the center of the island receives an average of 444 inches a year, making it one of the wettest places on earth. But most of the rain falls at night and in the early morning, and is concentrated in the mountains—leaving the weather along the northern, eastern, and southern shores just about ideal, perpetually sunny and between 75 and 85 degrees. Though not unknown to tourists, Kauai is less populated and less developed than the other destination islands in the Hawaiian archipelago. Princeville Resort is situated near the hamlet of Hanalei on the north shore of the island on the grounds of a former sugar plantation and cattle ranch, with much of the property overlooking the bay of the same name.

OPPOSITE:
The Lakes nine
at Makai, with
the volcanic hills
of Kauai in the
background.

16
DESTINATION

If Robert Trent Jones, Sr.'s work on the Big Island helped establish Hawaii as a burgeoning golf destination, his namesake son's projects at Princeville laid the groundwork for Kauai to become a contender for the title of "Hawaii's best golf island." There were several courses on Kauai when Jones broke ground on the Makai course at Princeville (which opened in 1971); these included Wailua, perhaps the state's most beloved municipal course. The three nines at Makai—Ocean, Lakes, and Woods—took golf on the Garden Isle to a new level, in terms of both maintenance and design. With the opening of the Prince course in 1990, Jones upped the ante further, fashioning a challenging—for players of average ability, *tormenting*—design on slopes that career back and forth some 300 feet above the Pacific. Others soon followed; a short drive down the coast on one of Kaui's few main roads brings you to Kauai Lagoons, which includes Kiele, a memorable Jack Nicklaus layout; a few miles farther south, there's Poipu Bay Golf Course and Kiahuna, two Robert Trent Jones, Jr. tracks, and Puahea, Kauai's newest course.

The Prince Course, with its quasi-links sensibility, waterfall-backdropped greens, and potentially spirit-busting difficulty, hoards most of the Princeville-oriented ink when golf journalists are assigned a Kauai golf round-up piece. Many players, however, will find an equally inspiring, if not overall more enjoyable experience, on Makai. Writer Brandon Tucker put it this way on www.worldgolf.com: "For the resort golfer looking for those Hawaii coastline money shots, the Makai has more oceanfront holes running along the North Shore. The reason it's a more friendly play is that in most instances, a miss doesn't mean a lost ball or a triple bogey like on the Prince. The Makai has its share of tough shots, but it doesn't feel like a constant grind."

"I always loved the three original nines at Princeville," Amy continued. "They are all very different. The Woods nine takes you into the rainforest and exposes some breathtaking mountain views. The Lakes has a great finishing hole, a long risk-and-reward par 5 that wraps around one of the nine's two lakes. On the Ocean nine, you simply can't duplicate the views from number 7—especially later in the day, when the sun is going down." Along with the 3rd hole at Mauna Kea, the 204-yard par 3 7th on the Ocean course is among the most photographed golf holes in Hawaii. The Pacific crashes 200 feet below, ready to swallow up any right-leaning shots; from the back tees, players get a 360-degree view of the North Shore of Kauai.

There's certainly enough on the Garden Isle to keep the most hard-core golfers happy, but even the most impassioned linkster would be doing him/herself a disservice by not taking a few mornings or afternoons to take in the scenery. On the west side of Kauai there's the rugged Na Pali Coast, where jagged cliffs drop three thousand feet to the crashing surf. Na Pali is best experienced from the water, and Kauai Sea Tours offers both catamaran and zodiac excursions here; some trips include stops at secluded beaches. During the winter months, humpback whales that have migrated here from Alaska are present; in the summer, hardy souls can kayak the seventeen-mile Na Pali coastline in what National Geographic has called the second-greatest adventure in America. East of Na Pali is Waimea Canyon, which Mark Twain dubbed "the Grand Canyon of the Pacific." Waimea is one mile wide, ten miles long, and 3,600 feet deep; the play of light and shadows upon the canyon's striated umber and copper is astonishing. Helicopter tours— including a fly-over of the Mt. Wai'ale'ale Crater (weather permitting)—are a visitor favorite. All the rain that falls here results in an amazing display of waterfalls cascading some 3,000 feet along the walls of this extant volcano to the fern-covered crater floor below.

For Amy Alcott, the best way to experience greater Princeville is from a kayak. "You can rent a kayak and paddle along the Hanalei River, which flows gently into Hanalei Bay," Amy said. "There's a charming restaurant on the river, the Dolphin, where you can have lunch [fresh seafood is emphasized, though steaks are also available]. The river often has beautiful orange flowers (from the hau tree) on the surface, and they smell wonderful. When you reach the bay, you have the chance to snorkel with green sea turtles, which are very playful creatures."

AMY ALCOTT is one of the most celebrated women golfers in the modern era of the game. A member of the World Golf and LPGA Halls of Fame, Amy has a go-for-the-pin style that has won her thirty-two tournaments worldwide, including five majors, and earned her a reputation as one the finest and most creative shot-makers in the game. Amy has served as a corporate and product spokesperson for a variety of blue-chip companies and brands during her pro career and continues to engage audiences and golf galleries with her colorful personality at speaking appearances as well as corporate and charity golf events. Amy has worked on several golf course design projects, including Indian Canyons Golf Club in Palm Springs and Brick Landing Golf Club in Ocean Isle, North Carolina. She also has written several books, *Spiked Shoes: Golf Lessons, Life Lessons* and *A Woman's Guide to Golf*.

16

DESTINATION

If You Go

▶ **Getting There:** Princeville is near the tip of Kauai, roughly forty-five minutes from the Lihue Airport. Nonstop flights from Los Angeles and San Francisco to Lihue are available on United and American Airlines; other flights to Kauai go through Honolulu or Maui.

▶ **Course Information:** The Makai Course at Princeville (800-826-1105; www.princeville. com) consists of three nines (Ocean, Woods, and Lakes), each playing to a par 36. Green fees are $59 for eighteen holes.

▶ **Accommodations:** The recently opened Princeville St. Regis Resort (888-625-5144; www.princevillehotelhawaii.com) is on premises at Princeville. The Kauai Visitors Association (800-262-1400; www.kauaidiscovery.com) provides a comprehensive listing of accommodations on the Garden Isle.

DESTINATION 16

DRIVING THE DANUBE

RECOMMENDED BY **Jim Lamont**

The Danube River flows through the heart of central Europe, coursing past Budapest, Vienna, and some of the most memorable Bavarian scenery in southeastern Germany. There are opera houses, cafés, more than a few cathedrals and monasteries, and golf courses.

"In the early nineties, I'd been organizing themed trips for a company that specialized in luxury cruises," Jim Lamont began. "One trip might have an archaeological theme, another a history theme. In 1996, a new boat, the *River Cloud,* was launched. It was designed especially for cruising the great rivers of Europe—the Danube, the Rhine, and the Moselle. I was on board with the owners during one of its inaugural cruises, and someone suggested the possibility of doing a golf-oriented cruise on the ship. At the time I thought it was a bad idea, but said I'd look into it. I did some reconnaissance in Hungary, Austria, and Germany along the Danube, playing recommended courses and speaking to other players in the clubhouse after my rounds to learn what courses they liked best. A few weeks of research unearthed an interesting line-up of courses—not world-renowned, but worthwhile. It might not be the trip for younger players who only care about golf, golf, golf—but it could appeal to more seasoned golf enthusiasts who are looking for a multi-dimensional golf travel experience."

Jim's instincts were correct. Before the first Danube River Golf Cruise (in the fall of 1996) had launched, the 1997 cruise had sold out.

For linksters with an interest in European history and epicurean delights, the Danube River Golf Cruise may be the perfect blend of golf, sightseeing, and conviviality. During the eleven days of the cruise (beginning or ending in Budapest, Hungary), the *River Cloud II* (sister ship to the original *River Cloud*) is transformed into a floating country club. This

is not the casino-lights-flashing/all-night-buffet cruise ship of the variety that haunts the Bahamas and Cancun. The *River Cloud II* has just forty-two elegantly appointed cabins for a maximum of eighty-four guests, with a design that fuses 1930s styling with all the modern amenities one could hope for. "The ship is old-style Europe, a Ritz-Carlton on the river, with European standards of service and cuisine," Jim continued. "We customize menus and wine lists to use local foods and vintages as much as possible. We host wine tastings with local vintners who will bring their best bottles on board, wines you probably can't find at home. Each cruise has a host from the golf world—movers and shakers like Peggy Kirk Bell (of Pine Needles fame) and Claude Brusse (director of golf at Yeamans Hall Club in Charleston). I think that part of the pleasure of the trip is traveling with a like-minded group of people. When guests sit down at dinner, they realize that there's a connectedness. The group size is optimal—it's a good number for shotgun starts, and a good number from a social perspective, as with a group of eighty, there's always someone you haven't met yet."

For trips that begin in the east, players fly in to Budapest. After a day of touring the twin cities of Buda and Pest (or resting from the overnight flight), you'll make your first golf stop at Pannonia Golf and Country Club, the finest of Hungary's seven (as of this writing) courses. Designed by Canadian Doug Carrick, Pannonia rambles through rolling farmland in the Mariavolgy Valley outside the city and recalls an American parkland design. (This is true of most of the courses along the Danube; the links associated with the British Isles are not found here!) The grounds of Pannonia once belonged to the Hungarian branch of the Hapsburgs, and the ornate clubhouse where you'll dine after golf once housed a greenhouse. After another day in Budapest (where one can visit Heroes Square or stroll the City Market), you'll board the *River Cloud II* and begin the cruise west toward your next port, Vienna. There will be a chance to tour some of the city's most venerable landmarks (like the twelfth-century St. Stephen's Cathedral) and immerse yourself in its vibrant café culture; for those with a sweet tooth, a trip to Hotel Sacher for a sampling of its namesake jam-filled chocolate torte is a must.

Over the three days in Vienna, guests enjoy two golf days. One outing is at the Fontana Golf Club, widely considered Austria's finest track, with finely manicured fairways and mountain vistas. Fontana has been a recent stop on the PGA European Tour. The second outing is at Colony Club Gutenhof, Austria's only thirty-six-hole complex. Jim likes to put his guests out on Gutenhof's East Course, which is set among bucolic century-old forests

OPPOSITE: Golf Club am Mondsee in Austria, just five minutes away from the Von Trapp house of Sound of Music *fame.*

17

DESTINATION

that are crisscrossed with streams. Following this round, guests are treated to a uniquely Viennese spectacle—a rehearsal of the Lipizzan stallions at the Spanish Riding School.

By the time the *River Cloud II* pulls out of Vienna, guests have settled into a comfortable routine. Full breakfast is served beginning at 7 A.M.; a lunch buffet is also set up so you can pack a box lunch for either the course or the day's tours. If it's a golf day, you'll leave the ship by 8:30—two coaches will be waiting to spirit you to the day's course. When you arrive at the course, there's a half hour to warm up on the range or putting green, then a shotgun start. At the round's conclusion, there's time to enjoy a drink in the clubhouse before catching the coach back to the boat. Afternoon historical or cultural tours are available, or you can grab a bicycle and go for a ride along the Danube. Cocktails are served at 6:30, sit-down dinner at 7:30. "While guests are welcome to dine in town, most opt to stay on the ship," Jim added. "Frankly, the food is better on board."

A favorite course on the Danube excursion comes on the second day in Germany, in the charming hamlet of Regensburg. "Sinzing am Minoritenhof is the only course on the itinerary that adjoins the river," Jim explained. "The course has built a small ramp that they only take out when the boat arrives. The day we play Regensburg, the captain comes on the public-address system and announces that the boat is having some problems, and we'll have to pull over; this allows us to skirt German river navigation rules that might otherwise prevent our stopping." Five of the holes skirt the Danube, allowing you the opportunity to incur a penalty by dumping a ball in one of inland Europe's most important waterways.

One of the charms of a golf expedition on the Danube is a chance to catch a glimpse of the Europe of yesteryear. This sometimes provides logistical challenges, as Jim Lamont explained: "Most of the courses we visit don't have golf carts, and as some of our guests like to ride, we feel it's important to provide them. So we have a small caravan—two tractor trailers filled with golf carts, and a moving van with guests' clubs—follow us along the route by land. When we arrive at the course, the carts are already waiting, conveyed by our drivers—big, burly fellows who work as truck drivers the rest of the year, and love this duty—with clubs already in place. In the early days, we'd be hesitant to have the carts brought into Hungary, as we weren't sure how long customs might hold them up when it came time to head back to Austria. The management at the course we were playing outside Budapest at that time felt bad, and they'd hire kids from the neighboring villages to come and pull trolleys for our clients. We'd arrive, and there would be a ragtag army of fifty children waiting to pull trolleys. Our guests loved getting their picture taken with the troupe of trolley pullers."

JIM LAMONT is president of Kalos Golf, which offers luxurious golf cruises to destinations in Europe and New Zealand.

If You Go

▶ **Getting There:** Danube River Golf Cruises begin or end in Budapest, Hungary, and conclude in Nuremberg, Germany, or Salzburg, Austria. All cities are served by many major carriers, including Lufthansa (800-399-5838; www.lufthansa.com).

▶ **Course Information/Accommodations:** The courses visited on the Danube River Golf Cruise vary, depending on the specific trip's itinerary. Six rounds are included. All cabins on the *River Cloud II* have a river view, are air-conditioned, and include a phone and television. All on-board meals (including wine) are included. Prices begin at $7,985 per person, based on double occupancy.

DESTINATION 17

THE GLEN CLUB

RECOMMENDED BY **Josh Lesnik**

Question: Where was the first eighteen-hole golf course built in America?

In New York, somewhere on Long Island?

In the sandhills of North Carolina, around Pinehurst?

Try again—it was just west of the city of Chicago, in the town of Belmont. The year was 1893, the course was the first incarnation of the Chicago Golf Club, and its creator and most energetic booster was Charles Blair MacDonald. MacDonald hailed from a wealthy Chicago family and attended university at St. Andrews in Scotland, where he befriended Old Tom Morris and fell in love with the game of golf. He became well versed in all aspects of the game—equipment manufacturing, architecture, and playing (he was U.S. Amateur champion in 1895), and the enthusiasm he brought back to the Midwest helped make greater Chicago an important early golf outpost in the United States. Many venerable golf clubs sprang up in the wake of Chicago Golf Club (which relocated in 1894 to its current location in Wheaton)—Butler National, Medinah, and Olympia Fields, to name a few. Chicagoland also has an abundance of fine facilities open to the general public—some 500 courses in all, including the Glen Club, which opened in 2001, yet harks back to an earlier time.

"There are so many great old private clubs around Chicagoland," Josh Lesnik said. "The Glen Club is built on the tradition of these old clubs. When you enter the grounds and the clubhouse, you feel like you're discovering something special."

The Glen Club, with its 195 acres of meandering streams, valleys, and copses of mature pines and catalpa, is a surprising sanctuary in the suburb of Glenview on the North Shore, just fifteen miles from the hubbub of the Loop. It's even more surprising when you realize that until 1995, the grounds of the Glen Club (and 800 surrounding

OPPOSITE:
It's hard to believe
that the grounds
of the Glen Club
were once part
of a naval air
station.

18

acres) were the site of the Glenview Naval Air Station, which operated seaplanes on nearby Lake Michigan, as well as antisubmarine planes. The land here didn't lend itself to a first-rate parkland course in its unadulterated state. To help make this happen, the course's developers, KemperSports (which oversees operations at more than one hundred courses throughout the U.S.) brought in Tom Fazio, an architect who's been known to move a bit of dirt around to realize his vision. "When you consider the location of the Glen Club, you expect flat terrain," Josh continued. "It's actually quite contoured. Fazio brought in two million cubic yards of dirt and 4,000 trees. You'd never know that much of the back nine was built on a runway. (Before the course was built, the base had an elevation variance of three feet; post-Fazio, some holes have as much as forty feet in elevation change.) The last two hours of your round, you're in the center of a natural haven, surrounded by blue herons, egrets, and rolling terrain. I think Tom did a great job in capturing the spirit of the old clubs of Chicago. When I walked the course with Tom Doak, he stood on the 7th green and said it reminded him of a MacDonald green at Chicago Golf Club. While the fairways are wide enough to give the average player a good level of satisfaction, there's plenty of challenge from the back tees for the guys playing the Nationwide Tour event or the Illinois Open that's been held here."

Josh related the experience of a round at the Glen Club. "I always feel that if I survive the first seven holes, I can start to score a bit. Six and 7 are long par 4s, as much golf hole as you'd want anywhere. The fourth is a short par 3, maybe forty feet downhill. The green is surrounded by fescue-covered hills. It's fun to hit a big downhill shot. Though the moniker 'Windy City' really comes from the bluster that our politicians can generate, the wind can blow on this hole and make club selection tricky. The 8th hole is a favorite, a short dogleg left par 4. There's a creek that meanders along on the left side of the fairway, eventually emptying into a lake. You don't necessarily need a driver off the tee, but you need to be accurate. On the back, the par 5 14th is reachable in two strokes if you risk flying the fairway bunker on the left. The green here is surrounded by huge old trees; one holds an owl's nest. Number 16 is an uphill par 4, with a challenging approach shot to a two-tiered green. You get the feeling you're playing a hilly course, which is an odd sensation for Chicago."

Part of the appeal of the Glen Club is the nostalgic touches that speak to old Chicago golf. The clubhouse is home to the Illinois Golf Hall of Fame, which features plaques and exhibits for each member, including Charles Blair MacDonald, Chick Evans (the first player to win both the U.S. Amateur and U.S. Open in the same year, who later established the Chick Evans Caddie-Scholar Fund), and PGA Tour winner D.A. Weibring. The 48,000-square-foot clubhouse features a grand ballroom and twenty-one overnight rooms for visiting golfers. "The rooms are named after old clubs in Chicago," Josh added, "and are decorated with black-and-white photos of the clubs. The food and service at The Grill is memorable. Overall, the Glen Club has a very old-fashioned feel. Though it's a public course, it has the ambiance of an old private club." In keeping with the past, the course has instituted a caddie program (rare for a daily-fee course), which has been an important element of Chicago golf since the days of Chick Evans.

JOSH LESNIK is the president of KemperSports. From 1998 through 2000, Josh spearheaded the opening and operation of Bandon Dunes Golf Resort in his role as the resort's general manager. He also served as the pre-opening and first-year general manager of the Glen Club. In his previous post at KemperSports, he served as vice president of marketing. Josh holds a Bachelor of Arts degree from Drake University and a Master's degree in marketing from Roosevelt University.

If You Go

▶ **Getting There:** The Glen Club is in Glenview, Illinois, conveniently located near O'Hare and Palwaukee Airports.

▶ **Course Information:** The Glen Club (847-724-7272; www.theglenclub.com) plays 7,149 yards from the back gold tees to a par 72; slope rating is 138. Green fees range from $105 to $175, depending on the season.

▶ **Accommodations:** The Glen Club (847-724-7272; www.theglenclub.com) has twenty-one rooms available for guests; stay-and-play packages are available. If you decide to stay in the city, the Chicago Convention and Tourism Bureau (877-244-2246; www.choose-chicago.com) provides an overview of accommodation options.

18 DESTINATION

NIRWANA BALI GOLF COURSE

RECOMMENDED BY **Bob Harrison**

A side trip to Bali may not fit easily into the typical Scottish or Irish golf travel itinerary. But for a golfer heading as far afield as Australia (perhaps to play Kennedy Bay or Barnbougle Dunes)—or if you happen to owe a significant other a romantic tropical idyll—a trip to Nirwana is in order. Here, in close proximity to the sacred Tanah Lot sea temple, you'll find steep volcanic mountains, pristine beaches of white and black sand, warm Indonesian hospitality, and a golf course that's likely to exceed all of your expectations, especially given its position far off most golfers' radar.

"We were given a fantastically dramatic piece of land to work with at Nirwana Bali," Bob Harrison began. "The possibilities presented by the land along the ocean were immediately evident. Our great challenge, from a design perspective, was how to treat the inland holes. They couldn't be a letdown after the coastal holes, or the overall experience of playing the course would be greatly diminished."

Bali is one of thirty-three provinces of Indonesia, lying just to the east of Java, and a few degrees below the equator. Sun worshipers and scuba divers have helped sustain a significant tourism trade, though agriculture—specifically the cultivation of rice—still plays a significant role Bali's economy. Rice also plays a role in the layout of Nirwana, which rests on the southwest coast of Bali, roughly forty-five minutes from the international airport at Denpasar. "Incorporating rice terraces into the design seemed a natural way to give the course a distinctly Balinese flavor, and to give some of the landscape away from the ocean visual interest," Bob continued. "Before we decided to build the terraces into our design, I traveled around Indonesia to see if this had been done before. I found a few venues where terraces had been used ornamentally around trees, but no place where they'd been integrated into the landscape as part of field of play. After we

OPPOSITE:
If the wind
is right, big
hitters can tempt
fate and go for
the green on
the par 4 13th
at Nirwana.

completed the shaping of the course, we dug the basic dimensions of the rice terraces with bulldozers, then local farmers came in and finished them off by hand. All the paddies on the course, I should mention, are operated as proper rice-growing operations. Rice plants have a very different appearance at different stages of growth, and we asked the farmers if they would be willing to plant rice in rotation in different parts of the course. They were happy to do so, and thus visitors see the terraces in different stages of their evolution as they make their way around." Rice terraces come into play on your first shot at Nirwana, as they cascade down the incline between the tee box and the first fairway and border the left side of the fairway on this 383-yard dogleg left. Take in the stark black mountains in the distance before you hit your approach and descend to the jungle-enshrouded green. (There are nearly seventy-five acres of rice terraces on the grounds of Nirwana, and proceeds from rice cultivation are shared among the farmers.)

Sporadic rice terraces certainly differentiate Nirwana from your average resort course, as do the many temples that are scattered throughout the property. "A few of the temples are fairly large, one the size of a small cottage," Bob explained. "There are a large number of smaller temples. The design of the course had to both preserve the temples and make them accessible by foot, as they are still in use by the local citizens." Novelties like rice terraces and active temples of worship should not distract visitors from the sound strategic design that lies at the heart of this track. "Despite the omnipresence of the jungle, the playing area is generally very wide," Bob continued. "The property has lots of natural gulleys and attractive little creeks, not to mention a great deal of contour. That gave us a lot to work with. On many of your tee shots, there are subtle rewards to be had from landing in the right part of the fairway—a more level lie, or a shorter shot to the green. On some of the tee shots, the reward for a sound shot is more obvious—you're not in the water!"

Though Greg Norman and Bob Harrison have done an excellent job of making the interior holes intriguing and exciting, the three holes perched along the cliffs above the Indian Ocean are hard to eclipse. The 214-yard 7th is the first of the oceanside holes, and perhaps the most dramatic. From a tee box that projects into the sea, your tee shot must carry the entire length of the hole (over a beautiful beach), to a green that's perched on a cliff. The green complex mimics the site of the Tanah Lot temple, which rests on a monolithic rock several hundred yards down the coast. The 14th hole is a 186-yard par 3 that plays across a headland, in the opposite direction from the 7th hole. Though they bear great similarities, the 14th is a bit more forgiving than the 7th, offering players a bailout area to the left. The preceding hole, a 335-yard par 4 13th, hugs the cliff line. "If the wind is right, big hitters may be able to drive this hole," Bob said, "if they're willing to carry some water. However, there's plenty of fairway west of the Indian Ocean for those opting for a less dangerous play, though from here, the approach to the narrow green can be intimidating."

With its dramatic vistas, strategic quandaries, and potential for sheer shot-making pleasure, Nirwana Bali is the kind of course you can play at least several times—and if you've come this far, you're likely to do so. Le Meridien (the resort associated with the course) offers extensive spa treatments to soothe sore muscles.

BOB HARRISON is vice president of Greg Norman Design, where he acts as Norman's design partner in Australasia. He has worked on the design of all the company's Australian projects, including the National Moonah Course, The Glades, The Grand, Pelican Waters, Brookwater, The Vintage, Sanctuary Lakes, and Kerry Packer's private course at Ellerston. A twenty-plus-year veteran of the company, for ten years Bob was also a director of Medallist, Greg's joint-venture golf-development company with Macquarie Bank. He is a member of the Society of Australian Golf Course Architects.

If You Go

▶ **Getting There:** Nirwana Bali is forty-five minutes from the international airport at Denpasar, which is served from Los Angeles by a number of carriers, including China Airlines (800-227-5118; www.china-airlines.com) and Cathay Pacific (800-233-2742; www.cathaypacific.com).

▶ **Course Information:** Nirwana Bali (+62 361 815 960; www.nirwanabaligolf.com) plays 6,805 yards from the back tees, with a slope rating of 131. Green fees are $175. This rate includes mandatory cart and caddie (caddies are charming Balinese women). May through September tends to have the driest weather.

▶ **Accommodations:** Le Meridien Nirwana Golf and Spa Resort (800-543-4300; www.starwoodhotels.com/lemeridien) offers many amenities. Rooms range from $120 to $250 a day.

ENNISCRONE GOLF CLUB

RECOMMENDED BY **John Steinbach**

There is always much excited whispering in golf travel circles about the latest hidden destination that's on the cusp of being discovered. Ireland hardly qualifies for this designation. As golf travel to Scotland exploded in the 1990s, savvy golf travelers began to explore and appreciate the many classic links of the Emerald Isle—and the relative afford-ability of Irish golf travel.

With the twentieth century drawing to a close, Ireland's economy enjoyed a tremen-dous surge, transforming the country from one of Europe's poorer nations to a position among its wealthier members. And Americans now flock in droves to play Waterville, Ballybunion, and Lahinch—and to plunk down green fees approaching $500 to play Old Head (see page 99).

You might say that Ireland is the new Scotland.

But as the highlands region of Scotland has been insulated from the minibus masses of conquering eightsomes by its remoteness, so the northwest of Ireland has been spared both the onslaught of visitors, and the subsequent homogenization of experience that can result from catering to too many of said visitors. The greater-known among the lesser-known (to paraphrase a former U.S. secretary of defense) include County Sligo Golf Club at Rosses Point, Ballyliffin, and Carne. One that you may not have heard of, but will almost surely be hearing more about, is Enniscrone.

"I was on my honeymoon in Ireland with my wife, Melanie," John Steinbach began. "We were staying at an inn in Ballycastle (County Mayo) that's owned by an old friend of mine, Terry McSweeney. I'd heard about Enniscrone from some of my TaylorMade col-leagues in Europe, and Terry noted that it was only forty minutes away, so we made the trip. Everyone at the clubhouse was very accommodating—that's something I've always found wherever I've played in Ireland. We engaged a caddie named Eddie—as colorful a character as you'd hope to find, with a sparkle in his eye and a few missing teeth—and off we went. The first hole is very flat and straight. It resembled a driving range, and I was wondering what all the fuss was about with this so-called hidden gem. But the second hole takes you off into the dunes, and from there on it's a whole different story."

Enniscrone rests in the southwest corner of County Sligo, just south of the town of the same name, overlooking Killala Bay. Like so many golf clubs here and in neighboring Great Britain, Enniscrone has a long history, and reached its current incarnation in fits and starts. A golf club was formed in Enniscrone in 1918, and competitions were held at three different locales on casually laid-out tracks around town through the twenties. Nine holes were laid out in 1930 and Enniscrone had a formal home, where the fairways were maintained by a horse-drawn mower. The club's membership waxed and waned over the next forty years, but by the early seventies, interest (and resources) had increased enough to allow the club to lease land in the dunes on the mainland and retain Eddie Hackett, Ireland's most celebrated architect, to create a championship-level eighteen-hole links. Hackett's best-known layout is Waterville in County Kerry, but he cut a wide swath in the northwest, laying out Ceann Sibeal, Carne, Donegal, and Rosapenna, in addition to Enniscrone. All in all, Hackett had his hand in eighty-five original designs and remodels, all in Ireland; that he's not better known outside of Ireland is not a reflection of his talent, but a function of his mild-mannered and self-effacing nature.

Eddie Hackett's reimagined Enniscrone was unveiled in 1974 to near-universal acclaim (at least across counties Sligo and Mayo and the few other hamlets that knew of its existence). Three years after Hackett's death, in 1999, modern English master Donald Steel was commissioned to exploit the possibilities of some dunes land adjoining the Hackett layout. The result was a rerouting of the course, with six holes on the less inter-esting flat land of the old layout replaced with six new holes in the dunes.

Whether you are peering out at the Atlantic from its many elevated tees or hiking through its brilliant green-tinted dunes, Enniscrone offers myriad pleasures. The mag-nificent 556-yard par 5 2nd hole—"Kilcummin"—offers unforgettable ocean views as you make your approach to the seaside green. The short par 4 number 13, "The Burrows," is one of Eddie Hackett's gifts to the course. From the tees overlooking the estuary of the River Moy, there's a classic blind first shot to a narrow fairway that's bounded by rolling dunes and replete with the humps and hollows that may send the perfect shot into the

deep rough—or redirect the wayward shot into a premium position. If you find the short stuff, it's a short-iron to a green guarded by deep bunkers.

"Enniscrone was a pure pleasure, with the long views and idiosyncratic bounces you expect from an Irish links course," John continued. "But what made the round so memorable for us was Eddie, the caddie. He knew every inch of the course, and delighted in pointing out landmarks in the hills and across Killala Bay—though we had the impression that he probably had never traveled to those places, or perhaps even outside of Enniscrone. His brogue was delightful—when calling out yardage to the pin, 144 yards came out 'one-fardy-far.'

"Melanie and I invited Eddie to join us for a pint after the round, and he accepted—though only after showering and changing out of his work clothes into 'proper' attire. We were joined by the club pro and felt right at home. Before leaving, we asked Eddie if we could take his picture. He acquiesced, but he wouldn't smile, though he was certainly a happy soul. I think he felt shy because of his missing teeth."

JOHN STEINBACH began his career with TaylorMade Golf in 1982 as a regional sales manager. He's worked with the company for twenty-five years, serving as vice president of advertising and publication relations and later as TaylorMade-Adidas Golf's director of public relations.

If You Go

► **Getting There:** Enniscrone is roughly four hours from Dublin and Shannon, which have the most international flights. Knock—roughly an hour from Enniscrone—has air service from Dublin on Aer Arann (+353 818 210 210; www.aerarann.com) and many cities in Great Britain via Ryan Air (+353 1 249 7791; www.ryanair.com).

► **Course Information:** Enniscrone (+353 96 36297; www.enniscronegolf.com) plays 6,948 yards to a par 73. Green fees range from €60 to €75.

► **Accommodations:** John Steinbach highly recommends the twelve-room Stella Maris Country House Hotel (800-323-5463; www.stellamarisireland.com) in Ballycastle, roughly forty minutes from Enniscrone. If you're seeking lodging closer to the course, Season's Lodge (+ 353 96 37122; www.seasonslodge.ie) is within walking distance.

OPPOSITE:
Enniscrone is one
of northwestern
Ireland's lesser-
known treasures.

20
DESTINATION

OLD HEAD GOLF LINKS

RECOMMENDED BY **Keith Baxter**

The Old Head of Kinsale is a startling peninsula that extends some two miles out into the Atlantic Ocean from near the bottom of Ireland. On the morning of May 7, 1915, Old Head played a small, sad role in World War I history; roughly eight miles off the peninsula, a German U-boat torpedoed the ocean liner *Lusitania*, which sank, taking the lives of 1,198 passengers and crew. Drownings still occur daily from April through September, but the fatalities are merely Titleists and Nikes.

And no one seems to mind.

"Old Head is a special place, indeed one of my favorite places," Keith Baxter began. "It's so exposed to the off-sea winds that they have to close it in the winter, as it's unplayable. It's one of the more expensive rounds you'll play anywhere at €295—certainly the most expensive in Ireland. But if you're willing to dig very deep to do it once in your lifetime, you'll never forget it. I first visited a year after it opened (1997), while I was working for a large food retailer in England. One of my suppliers had a manufacturing plant in Cork. I convinced them that it would be a grand idea to get a corporate membership at Old Head—that way they could take me out there whenever I visited!"

Described alternately as a diamond, a heart, or a swollen thumb, Old Head was once the site of castles, churches, and the dwellings of medieval monks; ruins of these ancient edifices are scattered throughout the property's 220 acres. (One such relic is the Stone of Accord, a circular stone with a small hole in the center; married couples and tradesmen would link their fingers through the hole to renew their banns or business contracts.) An exclamation point on this remarkable promontory is the Old Head of Kinsale Lighthouse, which has been helping to steer seafarers clear of County Cork since the 1840s.

OPPOSITE:
The par 5 12th extends out on a finger of the Old Head peninsula. "You feel like you're on the end of the earth out there," Keith Baxter confided.

21

DESTINATION

Before its transformation to a golf course began, Old Head was used as grazing land for cattle and sheep. The land was sold in 1989 to Irish-American financiers John and Patrick O'Connor, who were able to envision a golf course on this rock-ribbed terrain; rumors circulated at the time that the land was sold in part because the farmer was tired of losing livestock off the cliffs! Building the course was no small feat, as thousands of tons of rock had to be carted away and tons of topsoil brought in. Instead of importing a star designer, the O'Connors assembled an architectural team that mixed local playing talent and solid design résumés. It included the late Eddie Hackett; Ron Kirby, an alum of Jack Nicklaus design; Liam Higgins, an Irish player active on the Champions Tour; Paddy Merrigan, an Australian architect; the late Dr. Joe Carr, Ireland's most successful international amateur player; and the construction leader, Haulie O'Shea.

"It is without a doubt one of the most exhilarating sites in the world where golf is played," Keith continued. "If you have any vertigo, you could be in trouble. You play right by cliff edges where it's 250 feet down to the water. There are seagulls flying below you, and waves crashing. The waves reverberate in the many caves that dot the bottom of the headland, making a great booming noise. Your trousers are flapping in the wind. It's a total sensory experience."

While even the most casual duffer whose experience of seaside golf is limited to a lakeside driving range would find it difficult to completely ruin the playing possibilities of Old Head, the O'Connors' design team did a fine job of getting the most from the site. The par 72 layout has eight par 4s, five par 3s, and five par 5s, with nine of the holes along the cliffsides—and the roiling Atlantic in sight from every stance (save from the depths of a bunker or two). Visitors have the opportunity to slice or hook the ball into the water while advancing north or south along the headland; even if you're hitting it unerringly straight, you may be unable to resist the temptation to tee up a tired ball on the 18th and take a swing toward Wales. "The back tee is perched up near the lighthouse at the very edge of the headlands," Keith added. "It's imperative to have a go and watch the ball soar!"

There are many descriptives for Old Head, almost all of them from the golfing community superlative and positive. "For me, the best holes are those that hug the cliff edges," Keith opined. "They have a real 'Wow' factor. The holes in the interior are a bit of a respite—a chance to catch your breath and make a few good scores. Despite the absence of dizzying cliffs, they're still thoughtful holes. Though many may think of Old Head as a links course because of its proximity to the ocean, Old Head is not a true links. It's not built on sand, there aren't large sand dunes on the property, nor is the sea lapping gently within touching distance. That's not to say that some holes don't have a links feel. The course has another special touch—standing stones are used as markers."

The two par 5s on the back stand out for most players; Keith's favorite is the 564-yard 12th. "This is when Old Head truly comes to life for me," he said. "It's so rugged, so wild, so windswept, a visual feast bar none. You feel like you're on the end of the earth." The 12th rambles out on a finger of cliff that extends out into the water. You're tempted to cut off a few yards on your drive by playing to the left side of the fairway, but any miscalculations will put you with the fishes. (You'd do well to think twice about searching for wayward shots; signs along the left rough in bright yellow bear the following warning: "You are strictly prohibited from proceeding beyond hazard lines.") As you head farther out onto the peninsula, the clifftop narrows, along with the fairway. Making a five on this hole is special.

KEITH BAXTER is the author of a series of *Top 100 Golf Course* books, including *The Top 100 Golf Courses of the British Isles* and *The Golfer's Notebook*. He's also the editor and managing director of the Top 100 Courses of the World website (www.top100golfcourses. co.uk). He's played more than 1,000 different courses worldwide and more than eighty of the Top 100 in Britain and Ireland. Keith is a member of the International Golf Travel Writers Association and his home course is Bovey Castle.

If You Go

▶ **Getting There:** Old Head is located thirty minutes from Cork International Airport, which is served by Aer Lingus (800-IRISH AIR; www.aerlingus.com) from the United States (via Dublin).

▶ **Course Information:** Old Head plays 7,159 yards from the black tees to a par 72. Green fees are €295 for eighteen holes, €490 for thirty-six holes. Carts are available, though the course operates an extensive caddie program and encourages walking.

▶ **Accommodations:** Old Head offers luxurious lodging overlooking the course. Many visitors enjoy staying in Kinsale, just a few minutes from the headland. The Kinsale Chamber of Commerce (www.kinsale.ie) provides an overview of lodging options.

DESTINATION 21

BOGOGNO GOLF CLUB

RECOMMENDED BY **Robert von Hagge**

The lake region of northern Italy conjures up many pleasing images for sophisticates seeking a respite from the demands of modern-day life: three-hundred-year-old villas along sparkling Lake Como, perhaps populated by handsome celebrities like George Clooney (who does keep a home on the lake in Carate Urio); charming bistros serving up rich risottos and lively Barbarescos pressed from Piedmontese Nebbiola grapes; and the twinkling Pennine Alps to the north along the border with Switzerland,.

An inviting getaway indeed, made even more promising by the presence of fine golf courses like Bogogno.

"I was addressing a conference in Monte Carlo, and was approached by a charming Italian named Renato Veronesi," Robert von Hagge recalled. "He was planning to develop some land northwest of Milan into a residential country club, with two courses—much like what we see in the United States, but a very radical concept for Italy. He had a long list of golf course architects whom he had considered for the project, but the short list was Jack Nicklaus and me. He invited me to come and visit the property. It had everything it needed to be something special. Acquiring the land had been quite a feat. Renato had patched together forty pieces of property from nearly that many landowners—some had been in their respective families since the twelfth or thirteenth century. We drew up some routing plans contingent on acquiring these parcels—all but one were eventually purchased."

Robert and his then assistant (now partner), Rick Baril, created two dramatically different layouts at Bogogno. The Del Conte eighteen has an inland links flavor, wandering over flattish terrain with the peaks of the Monte Rosa mountain chain framing many of the holes. The Bonora eighteen is a more traditional parkland layout, climbing through hillier

OPPOSITE:
The Monte Rosa
mountains (part
of the Alps) are
in view from
many holes at
Bogogno.

parts of the property. "Del Conte is a little more challenging than Bonora," Robert continued. "Bonora has wider fairways and more expansive openings to the greens. Our idea
here was to create a lovely walk, even if you didn't have a golf club in hand. To that end,
we created several streams that circulate through the woods, as the sound of water gur-
gling through the forest is quite pleasing. On both courses, we strove to bring the long
views of the Alps into focus as much as possible. Great backgrounds can make shots
unforgettable."

The romantic or epicurean in you may wish to linger in the bistros of the neighboring
hamlets—Bogogno and Cressa, among others—to feast on the region's unique cheeses
and decadent white truffles (some valued at over $1,500 a pound). "We had some of the
most marvelous meals of my life in those towns," Robert recalled, "and stayed in some
charming bed and breakfasts. One of our favorite little hotels—San Rocco—was in a town
on Lago d'Orta called Orta San Giulio. San Rocco is in a former monastery, and it's just
across the water from Isola di San Giulio, which houses a basilica of the same name,
parts of which date back to the tenth century." You'll do well not to become too sated or
too relaxed—there's more golf to be had. Palaza Arzaga, near Verona, has an eighteen-
hole layout (by Jack Nicklaus, Jr.) and a nine-holer (by Gary Player) on the banks of Lake
Garda. Golf Club des Iles Borromees, between the cosmopolitan city of Milan and Lake
Maggiore, offers up brilliant vistas of both the Ticino Alps and the Milan skyline. Closer
by, in Agrate Conturbia, is the golf club Castelconturbia, with three sets of nine laid out
by Robert Trent Jones, Sr. The weather in the region is clement enough to permit year-
round play, and it's quite conceivable to ski and golf on alternate days in the winter season. Golfing gourmands may find the best of both worlds with a Piedmont cooking
school/golf extravaganza that's been assembled by Wide World of Golf.

The opportunity to spend time with the people of the Piedmont is one of the great
pleasures of any visit to northern Italy. Robert had many chances for interaction, and
some of the most interesting were on the golf course itself—before it was done. "In our
design methodology, we don't get too granular with our board specs," Robert explained.
"We make most of our refinements on the ground, and spend a lot of time with the on-
site construction crew. It's the best way to communicate with the shapers, and to catalog
what the player's going to experience, shot by shot. When we started building the course,
many of the farmers and other people whom Renato had purchased land from followed
us about, taking note of everything we did. After all, we were changing the complexion of

the property that had been intertwined with their lives for generations, and they wanted to see if we'd be making improvements. Sometimes there would be as many thirty people following us. I speak no Italian and they spoke no English, so they got an interpreter. As we'd talk through a step in the construction process, the group would sometimes utter a collective "Oh!" Other times they'd clap. I'd share the sketches we'd made of given holes, and make copies afterward so they had something they could take home to help explain what was happening.

"When I visit Bogogno, I still sometimes see the same farmers who followed me around the course walking the country roads around the property."

ROBERT VON HAGGE was born and raised on a golf course. Before his seventeenth birthday, he had worked as a caddie, shop boy, caddie master, golf course maintenance crewman, assistant greens superintendent, assistant golf professional, and commercial illustrator for sporting magazines. In 1955 Dick Wilson, one of America's foremost golf course architects, employed him as an apprentice golf course designer, and by 1959 he had become a principal designer. By the end of 1962, when he started his own firm, he had been involved in all or part of the design of forty golf courses in the U.S. and abroad. Robert has created some of the world's most outstanding and award-winning courses, and has been responsible for the design, redesign, or partial design of more than 250 golf courses in the U.S., the Caribbean, and sixteen foreign countries. He is a principal with the design firm of von Hagge, Smelek, and Baril.

If You Go

▶ **Getting There:** Bogogno Golf Club (+39 322 863 794; www.circologolfbogogno.com) is in the village of Bogogno, a short drive from Milan's Malpensa airport, which is served by most major carriers.

▶ **Course Information:** The Del Conte Course plays 6,780 yards to a par 72; the Bonora Course measures 6,749 yards from the back tees to a par 72. Green fees range from €72 to €150, depending on the season.

▶ **Accommodations:** One of Robert's favorite hotels around Bogogno is the Hotel San Rocco (+39 322 911 977; www.hotelsanrocco.it).

WHITE WITCH

RECOMMENDED BY **Rick Baril**

Among aficionados of golf course design, the Caribbean has not traditionally been viewed as a standout destination—this, simply because the sun and surf that make the islands so appealing on many other levels is hell to pay on turf grass. The challenges of growing and maintaining first-rate playing surfaces have historically discouraged many top-shelf designers and developers from doing adventurous work in the Caribbean. But agronomic advances, like the new turf hybrid Seashore Paspalum, are making golf more viable on the islands; the new hybrids require far less pesticide than other grass varieties, are salt tolerant, and can even be irrigated with brackish water. In short, the new grass is fueling a boom in new, high-quality courses.

White Witch, in Montego Bay, Jamaica, was in the vanguard of the Caribbean golf renaissance, opening for play in 2001. For Rick Baril, White Witch posed a once-in-a-lifetime opportunity, arousing both excitement and anxiety. "My first reaction to White Witch was nervousness," Rick said. "The site is spectacular—it's on the side of a mountain, with ridges and valleys cascading down to the ocean, all covered with dense vegetation. There are views of the Caribbean everywhere. The client—the late John Rollins (of Rolling Truck Leasing)—wanted us to create a landmark in Montego Bay, something special that people would recognize. He gave us huge swath of rugged, unusual landscape to choose from and let us run wild with it. Not to come up with an incredible end product would have been a great disappointment. That's where the nervousness came in."

White Witch takes its name from the former proprietress of the Rose Hall Plantation, Annie Palmer (no relation to Arnold), a figure from the 1820s whose history is hopelessly intertwined with Jamaican folklore. There are many variants on her tale—in short, it was believed that Mrs. Palmer was a practitioner of voodoo who dispatched of several husbands (including Mr. Palmer, who brought her to Rose Hall) when she became bored with them, and likewise murdered male slaves after taking them to her bed. Annie met an untimely, violent demise of her own, and some believe that her ghost still haunts the Great House at Rose Hall. There have been no reports of sightings of Mrs. Palmer at White Witch, though Rick was more than a little spooked by the original layout of the property. "The conceptual plan of White Witch showed the golf down in the valleys, and the houses on the ridges above. When I walked the valleys, I noted how narrow they were, and could picture the torrents of water that would come thundering through when it rained. If we put the course in the valley, all of our topsoil could end up in the ocean. So the decision was made to put the course at the top of the ridges. I can't imagine what this cost the developers in terms of the homes they might have built with multimillion-dollar views. But it certainly let us create a visually spectacular course."

With 600 acres of play area, each hole is isolated from the next, giving you a very private experience. Sixteen of the eighteen holes look out on the Caribbean, and somewhat remarkably, most of the holes play downhill. "There's really great pleasure to be had in hitting the ball from an elevated spot," Rick continued. "At White Witch, you get to hit many shots that put you at the top of the world. One of my favorites is the tee shot at number 1. The ball goes forever. Number 10 is another—it's a big par 5 dogleg left, and you can cut off as much as you dare if you can fly the ravine to the left." Elevated tees and downhill carries make for dramatic golf, but they don't translate into an easy track. While the fairways are ample, you need to find them, as the flora off the fairway can be thick to the point of impenetrable—"go off the fairway and you see teeth and eyes looking back at you," Rick joked. There are a number of jungle and/or ravine carries, and the wind—which is a thankfully cooling presence in the summer months—can make club selection tricky.

The most famous hole at White Witch—and one of the most photographed holes in the Caribbean—is the par 3 17th. The hole plays 195 yards from the back tees across a jungle chasm fronted by a handsome rock headwall to a green that's perched on a sloping ridge. "You come off the 15th green and take the cart path through the jungle," Rick described. "When you come out, you first witness the sea spread out before you—Cuba's eighty-five miles in the distance—then you notice a beautiful green that's surrounded by four bunkers. There's a tree in back of the green in the shape of an open umbrella that appears to be wonderfully manicured. In truth, the shaping comes from local cattle—the foliage is eaten back just as high as the cows can reach. The tee is thirty or forty feet above the green, so it's another hole where the ball seems to hang in the air indefinitely."

White Witch alone may be reason enough for many golfers to travel to Jamaica, but should you need more reasons, there are three others scattered around Montego Bay. These include the Tryall Club, once a venue for the Johnnie Walker classic; Half Moon Resort, a Robert Trent Jones, Sr. design that was recently updated by Jones's right-hand man, Roger Rulewich; and White Witch's sister course, Three Palms, operated by Wyndham. Beyond golf, there's a chance to drink in the island's beautiful beaches and laid-back, reggae-fueled vibe. "You can get a full dose of Jamaican culture in Montego Bay," Rick added. "Montego Bay is a party place, and the people are fun-loving and very friendly." If you feel that a little fright will enhance your travels, you can always opt for an evening visit to the Rose Hall Great House, which was painstakingly restored by Rollins.

RICK BARIL is a senior partner in the golf course architecture firm of von Hagge, Smelek, and Baril. Since joining the firm in 1982, he has designed courses in the United States, Mexico, France, Spain, Italy, Denmark, and Morocco. Rick's efforts have helped von Hagge, Smelek, and Baril garner its first-ever nomination for the Gold Medal Award for European Excellence.

If You Go

▶ **Getting There:** White Witch is near Montego Bay on the northwest side of the island of Jamaica. Montego Bay is served from the eastern United States by many carriers, including U.S. Airways (800-622-1015; www.usairways.com), American Airlines (800-433-7300; www.aa.com), and Air Jamaica (800-523-5585; www.airjamaica.com).

▶ **Course Information:** White Witch (876-518-0174; www.ritzcarlton.com) plays 6,859 yards from the back tees to a par 71; it has a slope rating of 139. Green fees range from $125 to $179, depending on the season. Green fees include caddie service.

▶ **Accommodations:** The Ritz-Carlton Golf & Spa Resort, Rose Hall (800-542-8680; www.ritzcarlton.com) has 427 luxurious rooms. Montego Bay is Jamaica's most popular tourist retreat; you'll find a list of other accommodations in the region at the Official Visitors Guide to Montego Bay, Jamaica (www.montego-bay-jamaica.com).

DESTINATION 23

HIRONO GOLF CLUB

RECOMMENDED BY **Ben Cowan-Dewar**

"When serious golfers begin a quest to experience the great courses of the world, their initial travels naturally take them to the United Kingdom and Ireland," Ben Cowan-Dewar began. "Once this appetite is sated, golfers tend to look further afield in their explorations. My own journey took me to Japan. While North Americans may sometimes think of Japanese golfers visiting the United States to play, we don't often consider Japan as a golf destination—though there are in fact a number of world-class venues there. On my trip, I played the Tokyo Golf Club, Kasumigaseki Course in Kanto, the very under-rated Naruo near Osaka, and the Fuji Course in Kawana, oft referred to as the Pebble Beach of Japan. My itinerary was leading to Hirono, which friends who had played it described as a masterpiece. Whenever a course is billed as truly elite, it can be pretty hard to meet expectations. However, Hirono did."

Golf came to Japan courtesy of an English tea merchant named Arthur Groom, who cleared enough land near his vacation home on Mount Rokko (near Kobe) to route a few holes at the turn of the last century. There was an eighteen-hole course on the site by 1904, which was quite popular with the British ex-pats (native Japanese citizens were excluded). At the same time, Japanese men who had worked or attended school abroad returned to their homeland with a passion for the game, and began campaigning for courses of their own. The first courses were primitive by overseas standards, and as more courses became available, golfers began calling for more inspired tracks. This demand helped deliver Charles Alison to the Land of the Rising Sun, and his three months there changed the direction of Japanese golf—though oddly enough, it was Harry Colt, not Alison, who was originally summoned. (Colt accepted the assignment for a then-princely sum of £1,500, but balked at the long trip and sent Alison in his stead.)

Being a partner of Harry Colt and Alister MacKenzie couldn't help but place Charles Alison somewhat in the shadows, though he was a great architect in his own right. Colt made Alison his man on the ground in America during the 1920s, where Alison produced such notables as Burning Tree (in Bethesda, Maryland), Country Club of Detroit, Sea Island (Georgia), Kirtland Country Club, Milwaukee Country Club, and Timber Point (Long Island). Born and educated in England and working extensively in the United States, Alison had a lot of exposure to great architecture, past and present. In a detailed profile of Alison on GolfClubAtlas.com, Thomas MacWood notes:

> Alison likely had seen more examples of great work than just about every other architect before or after him. He was able to watch Park, Colt and Fowler first hand transform the Heathlands into excellent golf. He was also able to watch contemporaries such as Ross, Tillinghast and Thompson produce some of their best and most influential works.

All these influences came to bear on Alison's brief sojourn in Japan, where he produced the original Tokyo Golf Club (which has since moved to the neighboring property at Kasumi), Kasumigaseki, the Fuji Course at Kawana, Ibaraki-Old, and his ultimate achievement, Hirono.

Hirono has been called the Augusta National of Japan, a moniker that speaks to both its exclusivity and its quality. ("The story is that there are many CEOs in Tokyo waiting for their invitation to play here," Ben quipped.) The parkland layout wanders through pine-covered hills and valleys, across gulleys and ravines. The prominent characteristics of Alison's design ethos are all evident at Hirono: large, deep bunkers, sideways-tilting greens, and prominent use of water hazards. (Alison, it's interesting to note, had an ambivalent relationship with water. He felt that it could often be a bad feature, since shots could not be played from a pond or stream, yet he frequently used water hazards. His notes show that he was sensitive to the significance of water in Japanese culture, and his employers' love of ponds and lakes, though he feared that "their love of water-hazards, were it not for their self-control, might develop dangerously.") The little par 3 5th hole at Hirono unites all facets of Alison's design. "The 5th is one of the world's great short par 3s," Ben continued. "It's not more than 150 yards and plays across a gully with water. Most of the front is guarded by bunkers—in Japan they call these deep bunkers 'Alisons' in homage to their creator—and the green angles sharply to the left. The course really gets its legs here. Hirono's only detractions come from the stylistic changes to Alison's original design, which has taken the rugged bunkering and softened it. The original photos of five are among the most visually arresting of any inland course with which I am familiar."

Other stunning one-shotters include holes 7 and 13 (the latter plays across a pond with a bridge, which brings to mind the 12th at Augusta). Two of Hirono's most revered holes come a bit later, at 14 and 15. "Hirono is a great driving course, and this is evident at the par 4 14th," Ben continued. "You play across the water to an uphill dogleg left. The fairway also slopes significantly to the left. If you play to the right, you're left with a long approach to the green. If you play too far to the left, you risk running off the fairway. I think Alison came up with a very inventive way to incorporate the slope into the hole. Number 15 is a 550-yard par 5 that requires you to play across two gulleys that create two distinct landing areas. There's a pine tree in the fairway on the fifteenth that can be reached with only a very solid drive; it's beloved by the membership, and has become the signature of the course."

Course experience aside, Ben noted the differences between golf in Japan and the U.S. "The game is quite similar throughout the world—with the possible exception of the pace of play. The entire event in Japan is quite different. Upon playing nine holes you retire for lunch. This is not a snack at the halfway house, but a proper lunch in the clubhouse—soba noodles, sushi, some sandwiches, and a few drinks, perhaps. After an hour, play on the back nine resumes. It's a wonderful part of the experience to sit down mid-round and get to know your hosts. The foreign nature of the experience continues after the round, with the bath ritual. I remember seeing a picture of some Japanese men sitting on upside-down buckets hand-bathing in photographer Brian Morgan's book of courses of the world. For some reason, I thought *that* was the bath. It's actually a *prequel* to the bath. At Hirono, the bath is a dead-calm pool of scaldingly hot water that looks out on a beautiful garden. As a North American guest, I felt obliged to stay in longer than my host . . . even as heat stroke set in!"

BEN COWAN-DEWAR founded Golf TI in 1999, when his passion for the game impelled him to leave the finance world. While establishing Golf TI, Ben kept his feet on the ground by managing a golf marketing consulting business, and worked for clients in twenty countries. He has planned and led Golf TI trips to destinations as diverse as

Australia, Indonesia, France, and Dubai. Scouting the world's best courses has taken Ben across five continents, and he sits on the *Golf* magazine panel that establishes the authoritative rating of the world's finest courses. He is a partner of the acclaimed golf architecture website GolfClubAtlas.com and is currently building a seaside course in Eastern Canada, Cabot Links. Having traveled to more than thirty countries over the last ten years, Ben's preference is to be at home in Inverness with his wife and son.

If You Go

▶ **Getting There:** Hirono Golf Club is on the outskirts of Kobe, which is convenient to the airports in Osaka. Osaka is served from San Francisco and Los Angeles by many carriers, including United (800-864-8331; www.united.com), U.S. Airways (800-622-1015; www.usairways.com), and ANA (800-2FLY ANA; www.ana.co.jp).

▶ **Course Information:** Hirono (+81 794 85 0123) plays 6,925 yards from the back tees. Hirono is extremely private, but players from abroad can occasionally gain access by traveling as part of an organized golf tour. Luxury golf tours that include play at Hirono are available from several companies, including Golf TI (866-866-9295; www.golfti.com).

▶ **Accommodations:** The official Kobe tourism site (www.feel-kobe.jp) highlights accommodations around the region. You can research lodging options in the nearby larger city of Osaka by visiting the Osaka Visitor's Guide (www.osaka-info.jp).

24

DESTINATION

CONGRESSIONAL COUNTRY CLUB

(BLUE COURSE)

RECOMMENDED BY **Robert Morris**

Contrary to what some might think, Congressional Country Club is not a haven for members of the United States Senate and House of Representatives.

It's much more exclusive than that!

Robert Morris feels fortunate to be a member, and has seen the club from many different sides. "I waited about a dozen years to get in, but already knew many of the members before joining," Robert began. "As a boy I caddied out there. Much later, I served as a member of the board of directors, and oversaw merchandising activities when the U.S. Open was held there in 1997. For me, Congressional Country Club has a rare combination of fine aesthetics and great playability. The allure of the place begins when you drive through the gates. There's the picturesque, old, established clubhouse, and the lovely landscaping around the grounds. Before you even get to the range, you know you're in for something special. That the course can meet the expectations set is a testament to its excellent design. Every aspect of shot making is required to play the course well—you need finesse, power, the ability to move the ball left to right and right to left, play uphill and downhill lies."

While not *strictly* a playground for elected officials, Congressional does have roots on Capitol Hill. Congressmen Oscar E. Bland and O.R. Luhring of Indiana helped found the club in 1924, envisioning a place where titans of industry and congressmen could fraternize in a convivial atmosphere. (In a nod to its roots, Congressional's tee markers are fashioned in the shape of Capitol buildings.) There would be two eighteen-hole tracks—the Blue and the Gold. Devereaux Emmet, a scion of one of New York's most prominent families and craftsman of several classic designs in the Empire State (including Garden City Golf Club and Leatherstocking Country Club), was brought south to design the first

113

nine holes on each course. Little of his original work remains, as Donald Ross came north from Pinehurst to revise the course in 1930—and Ross was followed by Robert Trent Jones, Sr. in 1957, and then Rees Jones some thirty years later. The work of the Joneses Senior and Junior was largely devoted to toughening up the Blue for coming majors. The course has been the site for two U.S. Opens, with a third slated for 2011. It has hosted the PGA Championship, the U.S. Senior Open, the U.S. Women's Amateur, and U.S. Junior Amateur; it's also now the site of the AT&T National hosted by Tiger Woods.

"I think a good golfer will truly appreciate the design qualities of Congressional," Robert continued. "The landing areas are very fair—so if you're driving the ball well, it will set up for scoring. If you're not driving well, there's trouble on the left and right; if you're not executing, you'll be punished. At times it feels like a big tiger staring you down, saying 'Try again, we're not going to let you get away with that shot!' Rees [Jones] did some interesting things with the green complexes. The target areas in front were made narrower with encroaching bunkers, while at the back of the greens, the target was made bigger. You want to hit into the center or back of the green, as the trouble is lurking in front. The greens are shaped so you can tuck pins into nooks and corners—they're a shot maker's dream."

When asked to name a favorite hole at Congressional, Robert paused. "There are eighteen beautiful holes and choosing even two or three favorites is a challenge. I'm very fond of the 2nd hole, a classic uphill power par 3. It's over 200 yards (235 from the back) and the front is guarded by six bunkers; a tongue in front kicks short shots into the sand. There's a great landing area at the back of the green; if you can stop a ball there, you know you've hit a well-executed shot. The 6th hole is a par 5 for member play and a long par 4 (518 yards) during professional tourneys. As a par 5, it's a wonderful risk/reward hole. The green is surrounded by a lake on the right side that's beautifully edged with stonework. If you go for this hole in two, you're either in the water or on the green. To me, this is a great testing point in the round. Many matches are lost here as players become unnerved by their second shot. Another favorite of mine is the 10th hole, which used to be the old par 3 18th. Many people didn't like the idea of the round ending on a par 3, so the routing was switched around and this hole was refashioned. It's a long par 3 across the biggest lake on the course, and there's an amphitheater feeling behind the green—a very TPC look."

For many players (and spectators at home) it is the 18th that signifies Congressional, a long par 4 (450 yards during professional matches) that plays downhill. "The fairway

OPPOSITE:
The 18th
(foreground)
and the 10th
(background) are
two favorites at
Congressional.

DESTINATION

25

moves from right to left, and is lined with white pines on either side," Robert described. "Ideally, you'll hit the right center of the fairway so the ball will take the slope. Water surrounds the kidney-shaped green, and leaks into half of the green complex on the left. There's a tendency to hook shots from a downhill lie, so it takes some nerve to hit into the left side when the pin is there. Those who aren't strong at heart can bail out to the right, though there are bunkers waiting there. If you do bail out and make it on, you have a long putt over a swale to the pin. I like watching people play this hole—are they bold and able to commit, or do they play safe and bail out? Play on this hole is very indicative of one's approach to the game."

One of Robert's most enduring memories of Congressional comes from his caddie days. "When they had the U.S. Open at Congressional in 1964, players weren't allowed to bring their own caddies, thanks to USGA rules. They had to use local caddies, who were chosen by a lottery draw. I was in the caddie pen on the first day of the tournament, and I got a call from the caddie master, Jocko Miller, a fellow with a boxer's build—he looked like a Coke machine with a head on it. I came out to the starter's area and he said 'Stand right here.' A Cadillac drove up, and out popped Arnold Palmer—I had drawn Arnold Palmer for the U.S. Open! The trunk opened and Jocko said, 'Boy, get those clubs.' Palmer had this huge Wilson bag with mink headcovers. I started pulling the clubs out, but the woods got caught in the bay of the trunk—and the clubs fell out of the bag. Jocko whacked me in the back of the head so hard I saw stars, and sent me back to the caddie pen. I was devastated. Later in the day I was called up again, and I ended up caddying for a fellow named Bob Charles, a left-hander from New Zealand. He had a distinctive accent, one that I'd never heard before, but we worked well together. He ended up finishing third in the U.S. Open that year, two places ahead of Palmer.

"Ten years ago, I was playing a tourney with Bob Charles [now Sir Bob Charles, New Zealand's most revered golfer] in Japan. I said 'Bob, you may not remember me, but I caddied for you in the 1964 U.S. Open.' We reminisced about that day more than thirty years ago, walking up the fairways in Japan."

ROBERT C. MORRIS is a cofounder of Billy Casper Golf and has served as its vice chairman since the firm's inception. He directs business development for BCG, focusing on the acquisition of management agreements. Robert is responsible for oversight of all marketing, sales, public relations, and player development efforts of the firm. He is an active participant in Golf 20/20 and other industry player development initiatives, and is a sought-after industry expert in the creative development and management of golf courses in an increasingly competitive environment. Prior to BCG, Robert managed the careers of several golf touring professionals and championship winners, including company namesake Billy Casper. An accomplished player, he has been ranked in the Top Fifteen senior amateur golfers worldwide.

If You Go

▶ **Getting There:** Congressional Country Club is in Bethesda, Maryland, just northwest of Washington, D.C.

▶ **Course Information:** Congressional (301-469-2000; www.ccclub.org) plays 7,250 yards from the tournament tees, to a par 72; it has a slope rating of 142. Should your congressman happen to be a member (or at least know a member) and able to secure you a tee time at this private enclave, green fees are in the vicinity of $160.

▶ **Accommodations:** Destination DC (202-789-7000; www.washington.org) provides an overview of lodging options in the nation's capital. Should you prefer to stay in Maryland, the Maryland Office of Tourism (866-639-3526; www.visitmaryland.org) lists accommodations around Bethesda.

DESTINATION

25

FARM NECK GOLF CLUB

RECOMMENDED BY **David Baum**

During the summers of the 1990s, golfers at Farm Neck Golf Club would frequently be treated to—or, depending on your point of view, tortured by—the spectacle of a sitting president and his entourage (entailing at least six golf carts bearing Secret Service agents, a police sniper, assorted aides, and someone holding the nuclear codes) playing a casual round of golf. While his responsibilities may have been somewhat reduced, this former governor of Arkansas still makes occasional forays to Martha's Vineyard to relax at this fashionable island escape. And when he decides to tee it up at Farm Neck, he's just another one of the eclectic characters you're likely to encounter.

"One of the things that has always struck me about Farm Neck is the diversity of its member base—racially, ethnically, socioeconomically—and the very low-key nature of the place, given the quality of the course," David Baum began. (Farm Neck is semiprivate, with limited tee times for nonmembers.) "Whether it's a foursome of Wall Street executives, a commercial fisherman, or Bubba himself—all the players at Farm Neck share a love of the Vineyard and a love of golf."

Once an important outpost for the whaling industry, the island of Martha's Vineyard (seven miles off the southwestern tip of Cape Cod, and only accessible by air or water) is best known for its popularity as a vacation retreat—especially for the rich and famous. Though a long list of moguls and celebrities maintain residences here (some have dubbed the island "Hollywood East"), the atmosphere is decidedly low-key. People—whether movie stars or maintenance men—come to enjoy pristine beaches, dependable sailing winds, and striped bass fishing, or simply to savor the views out over Nantucket Sound. Martha's Vineyard has a long history of live-and-let-live tolerance, evidenced by the long-standing presence of African-American and Jewish summer residents, who found acceptance here generations ago when other resort communities closed their doors. "Half of the thrill of playing at Farm Neck is just being on Martha's Vineyard," David effused. "Everything is so relaxed; wherever you go, you can be dressed in flip-flops, shorts, and a T-shirt."

All the serenity and New England seaside beauty are revealed as you make your way around Farm Neck—"It's no wonder that Bill Clinton (allegedly) chose to take countless mulligans here," David joked. "Farm Neck's natural beauty—from fields of wildflowers to exhilarating views from the holes that wind around Sengenkontacket Pond—is both breathtaking and remarkably relaxing." Farm Neck rests on a peninsula (or "neck," in local parlance) of rolling farmland on the eastern side of the island, overlooking Nantucket Sound. The course has an interesting provenance—the first nine were laid out in 1979 by Bill Robinson and Geoffrey Cornish. (Cornish's career, incidentally, began at Capilano outside Vancouver in 1935, when he evaluated soils for Stanley Thompson; he has since designed 230 new courses, with more designs in New England than any other architect.) A year later, a second nine was added, laid out by a little-known designer with a wonderful golf name—Patrick Mulligan. Some such piecemeal collaborations could provide a jarring golf experience, but most feel the two nines coalesce nicely. "The elevated par 3 4th hole is one of Farm Neck's most devilish tests due to a deep but narrow green that is difficult to hold, particularly when the wind is blowing—as it usually is," David continued. "The safe play is to the front of the green, but if you miss the mark, take heart in the exceptional view of brackish Sengenkontacket Pond and Nantucket Sound in the distance. If you're a movie buff, you may recognize the pond as the site where Bruce the shark was lurking near the son of Police Chief Martin in the movie *Jaws*."

While the front nine is quite pleasing, David prefers the back nine—providing you can get past the marauding crows that hover near the 10th green waiting to abscond with treats from the snack shop at the turn; regulars know to keep snacks zipped up in their bags. "The 11th, a banana-shaped par 5 dogleg, plays beside a field of wildflowers," David described. "The view from the tee is a sight to behold, though number 14, a short dogleg left that plays along Sengenkontacket Pond may be Farm Neck's beauty contest winner. A well-placed drive in the right center of the fairway opens up the green for the approach shot. The round closes with a 523-yard, severe dogleg-right par 5. While long hitters can get home in two, the threat of wetlands to the left, water in front of the green, and out of bounds on the right makes for a thrilling risk/reward finish."

The best finish, however, may come on a twilight walk along one of Martha's Vineyard's many beaches, breathing in the salty air as the sun disappears behind Cape Cod.

DAVID BAUM is the owner, publisher, and editor in chief of *Golf Odyssey: The Insider's Guide to Sophisticated Golf Travel*. Prior to purchasing the seventeen-year-old publication in 2005, he spent seventeen years in investment banking at Goldman Sachs. A long-time subscriber to *Golf Odyssey*, David jumped at the chance to shape a second career around his passion for golf and travel. David continues the *Golf Odyssey* tradition of providing expert, anonymous reviews of golf destinations throughout the world without the support of advertising. He recently published two books, *Planning the Ultimate Golf Vacation* and *Planning the Ultimate Bandon Dunes Golf Vacation*. Originally from Columbus, Ohio, David moved to the New York area after graduating from Indiana University.

If You Go

▶ **Getting There:** To reach Martha's Vineyard, you'll need to travel by sea or by air. Most travelers arrive via one of the ferries that service Martha's Vineyard, like the Steamship Authority (www.steamshipauthority.com), which sails from Woods Hole. Cape Air (800-352-0714; www.flycapeair.com) offers regularly scheduled flights from Boston, New Bedford, and Providence.

▶ **Course Information:** Farm Neck Golf Club (508-693-3057) plays 6,815 yards from the back to a par 72, with a slope rating of 135. Green fees range from $50 to $135, depending on when you visit. David cautions that it can be very tough to get out on summer weekends, and that for fine weather and uncrowded fairways, May and September can be excellent times to visit.

▶ **Accommodations:** The Vineyard offers many fine options. David likes the Hob Knob Inn (800-696-2723; www. hobknob.com), Winnetu Inn & Resort (978-443-1733; www. winnetu.com), and The Charlotte Inn (508-627-4151; www.relaischateaux.fr).

EL TAMARINDO

RECOMMENDED BY **Evan Schiller**

Mexico is the American golfer's second-most-popular golf destination off the mainland, next to Hawaii. Cabo San Lucas (at the southern tip of Baja California) has been a perennial favorite for Yankee visitors, but Cancún (on the Yucatán Peninsula) and Puerto Vallarta (on the Pacific, west of Guadalajara) are fast becoming golf vacation spots in their own right. Puerto Vallarta has eight courses as of this writing, including Jack Nicklaus's Punta Mita (at the Four Seasons Resort) and Robert von Hagge's El Tigre (at Paradise Village Beach Resort and Spa). While on assignment to photograph some of Puerto Vallarta's seaside splendors, Evan Schiller ventured a bit further off the beaten path to what he termed "a Fantasy Island–kind of isolated place"—El Tamarindo.

"I was playing a course in Palm Springs one winter, and saw a fellow wearing an 'El Tamarindo' golf shirt," Evan recalled. "I asked him if he'd played there, as I'd heard a little bit about it. He replied, 'Yes. I am one of the owners.' When I learned that I'd be heading to Puerto Vallarta, I contacted him, and he invited me to visit. It's about a three-hour drive from the city, and I was advised not to stop in the towns, as American visitors were uncommon and might attract unwanted attention. I drove through the jungle for three hours—there's no place to stop beyond the few towns I was advised against visiting—so I just kept going. Eventually, there was a gate with a guard. Passing the gate, a road made of cobblestone and tiles wound down through the jungle, with iguanas scurrying out of my path. After six miles, you reach the ocean and the resort—about as remote and private a spot as you can imagine, surrounded by the jungle and the beach."

Within a few minutes of arriving, most guests will see El Tamarindo as it seems to have been intended: an idyllic, upscale, honeymoon-style getaway. Twenty-nine thatched-roof *casitas* are spread along the beachfront and in the hills above. They're a picture of

south-of-the-border indolence, yet many sleek features—an ample master bedroom, an outdoor Jacuzzi and private plunge pool, and elegantly appointed bathrooms—make them quite sophisticated. You will not hear the whine of jet skis here, though hiking, mountain biking, kayaking, sailing, and windsurfing are encouraged. A host of spa services are all available within the 2,000-acre property, which includes two miles of private beachfront. This is not your typical buddy-golf-getaway kind of place, and at least on paper, the golf course seems an afterthought . . . though what an inspired afterthought!

El Tamarindo is fashioned—well, hacked and muscled—from the thick jungles that front the *Costalegre* at the southern edge of the Mexican state of Jalisco. While a tee sheet of forty or fifty players would be considered a busy day, no expense has been spared to create a golf experience that would draw players in droves, were it a bit closer to a population center—or even a modest population of somewhat affluent golfers. Perhaps David Baum summed it up best in *Golf Odyssey*: "There is not one flawed hole on this 6,682-yard, par 72 course, and no less than fourteen holes could qualify for signature status! Numbers 6, 7, 8, and 9 may be the best string of four holes in the world. Before dismissing this as an overstatement, try them."

After an opening two holes in the jungle, you step onto the 3rd tee and the Pacific reveals itself in the distance, through a sliver of fairway hewn from the native flora. The green of this 387-yard par 4 is flanked by bunkers, and adjacent to more inviting sands—namely, the beach. El Tamarindo's Beach Club is strategically located by the fairway, and players are encouraged to change into a bathing suit, dip in the ocean, rinse with a freshwater shower and return revitalized to the 4th tee, which leads back into the jungle. The meager number of rounds logged here encourages such dalliances. At hole number 8, a short par 4, you return to the ocean. "There's an elevated tee that looks out on the Pacific," Evan continued. "You have to carry a swatch of jungle to reach the fairway far below." The diminutive 9th, a downhill par 3 of 145 yards from the tips (and just 112 yards from the whites), will prove to be one of the most dramatic par 3s you'll play south of the border . . . or anywhere. "The tee is up high above the hole—at least a 75-foot drop from the back tees," Evan added. "The rocks off the cliffsides extend down along the left side of the green, waves from the Pacific are crashing to the right. At certain times of day, the shadow of a palm tree hangs over the putting surface." It's an exceptionally beautiful hole that yields a most satisfying golf shot, the kind of hole that you'd like to camp out on with a shag bag full of balls to while the day away.

OPPOSITE:
The par 3 12th at Tamarindo abuts the Pacific; some guests opt for a quick skinny dip after putting out.

DESTINATION

27

If you happily exhaust yourself on the 9th, you'll find comfort in the open-air snack bar at the turn. No hot dogs and Bud here; instead, there's fresh-made guacamole, ceviche (fresh fish salad), and a host of tequila treats. Again, players are encouraged to linger, as there are not likely to be any groups behind that you'll slow down. The par 3 12th is a highlight on the back. The green lies almost on the beach, and Golf Director Alberto Bertran says that many European guests will pause for a quick skinny dip—it's unlikely that there will be any voyeurs peeking from the trees. "The day I played," Evan said, "I was the only player on the course."

EVAN SCHILLER is a golf professional as well as a professional photographer. He has been invited to photograph hundreds of the finest golf courses around the world, including Pebble Beach Golf Links, Augusta National Golf Club, The Old Course at St. Andrews, and Ballybunion Golf Club. Evan's work has appeared in many national magazines, books, and calendars, including the *U.S. Open Magazine*, *The Masters Journal*, *The Ryder Cup Journal*, *Golf Digest*, *Golf* magazine, *LINKS* magazine, *Travel & Leisure Golf*, and the Jack Nicklaus Golf Calendar. His photography is also featured in the book *Golf Courses of Hawaii*. Evan is an officially licensed photographer for Pebble Beach Company and his photography is on display at the Images of Pebble Beach gallery at The Lodge at Pebble Beach. He has also competed in professional golf tournaments around the world and on the PGA Tour, including the U.S. Open.

If You Go

▶ **Getting There:** El Tamarindo is located in the Mexican province of Jalisco, roughly forty-five minutes north of Manzanillo International Airport. Manzanillo is served by many carriers, including Mexicana Airlines (www.mexicana.com).

▶ **Course Information:** El Tamarindo Golf Club (+52 315-35 150 32; www.eltamarindoresort.com) plays 6,682 yards from the back tees to a par 72; the slope rating is 132. Green fees are $165 for resort guests, plus $20 for a mandatory caddie.

▶ **Accommodations:** The resort has twenty-nine well-appointed *casitas*, though El Tamarindo's luxury comes dearly—guest rooms begin at $425 in the off-season and $565 during prime time.

EL CAMALEÓN AT MAYAKOBA

RECOMMENDED BY **Fred Funk**

When you already compete in thirty professional tournaments a year like Fred Funk, a new tourney had better be pretty special to attract your attention. "There are two considerations for a PGA Tour pro when evaluating whether or not to participate in an event," Fred explained. "On the competitive side, you look for a course that will reward the guy who is playing well that week. On the personal side, you look for a destination that would be a pleasant escape for the family. Mayakoba delivers on both counts. The first year (2007) that El Camaleón hosted a PGA Tour event (the Mayakoba Golf Classic), a lot of the guys on tour who didn't make the trip were very curious to hear about the course from the players who did participate. All the reviews were very positive, and in 2008, you had many more players competing."

Mexico's Yucatán Peninsula—the arm of land that extends north and east into the Caribbean Sea from the Central American nations of Belize and Guatemala—has become a favorite escape for winter sun-seekers. The region's largest city, Cancún, offers nonstop nightlife that's sure to appeal to spring-break-style revelers, and broad beaches for nursing the morning's inevitable hangover. Farther down the peninsula, hints of an older, calmer Mexico appear, though the tourism interests are expanding their claim along the Caribbean. These include the birth of many new golf resorts. "It used to be that Acapulco and Cabo San Lucas were *the* golf spots in Mexico," said Bill Hogan, president of Wide World of Golf. "Within the next ten years, the Mayan Peninsula will exceed those venues, thanks to the many fine new courses being built. In addition to El Camaleón, there's Moon Palace (a Nicklaus design), Playa Mujeres (another Norman design), and the Hilton Cancún. There are at least four more being built. The resorts around Cancún provide excellent quality and great value."

El Camaleón was created by Greg Norman Golf Course Design on a parcel of land that encompasses three distinct landscapes—tropical jungle, mangrove swamps, and seaside beaches; the contrasting settings inspired the course's name ("The Chameleon" in *inglés*), though an assortment of geckos and iguanas are certainly present on the grounds. The course is further distinguished by the limestone canals that meander through most of the layout, pulsing with clear, inviting water. The canals are testament to a geological phenomenon found through much of the state of Quintana Roo, on the eastern side of the Yucatán Peninsula. The surface strata consist of porous limestone, remnants of what was not so long ago (in geologic terms) an ocean floor. Over thousands of years, rainwater filtered through the limestone, creating an extensive series of underground rivers. At El Camaleón, the surface stratum has collapsed to expose the rivers. The Yucatán is also well known for its *cenotes* (pronounced "say-no-tays"), sinkholes providing entry to the cool underground rivers. In fact, a *cenote* graces the fairway of the 558-yard opening par 5 at El Camaleón; at 300-plus yards from the tee, it provides an excellent target for most of us. For the big straight hitter (or the duffer who badly misses his/her second shot), a shot in here will mean a stroke and a drop. (The Mayans revered *cenotes*, viewing them as portals to a spiritual world below the earth. At the nearby ruins of Chichén Itzá, divers have discovered jewelry, pottery, and human skeletons, believed to be offerings to the gods.)

"I think that Greg did a great job with the design," Fred continued. "It's hard to lay out a course that walks the line between being challenging for professional-level players and enjoyable for higher-handicappers, but Greg pulled it off. El Camaleón is a fun course to play, as it doesn't beat you up with its length. All the grass on the course is seashore paspalum, mowed at different heights for the greens, fairways, and rough. It has a very pristine look, and the playability is excellent. The ball really sits up, like you're hitting off carpet. While it's not particularly long, there's not a lot of room for error. If you stray far from the fairway, you may find yourself in the mangrove swamps, which come into play on many holes. The wind certainly comes into play, especially on the east/west holes—it's one of the defenses the golf course has against par."

The ever-changing landscape and constant presence of the canals (which attract abundant bird life) makes a round at El Camaleón a visual feast. For Fred, the track's par 3s stand out from a playability perspective. "I like the fact that they're not 240 or 250 yards—par 3s that long are not much fun to play. The 7th hole abuts the beach, looking right out to the island of Cozumel. It's only 125 yards, but the wind coming off the Caribbean makes

OPPOSITE:
El Camaleón's diminutive par 3 7th plays to the edge of the Caribbean.

DESTINATION

28

club selection tough. You need to figure out how to keep the ball out of the wind. Number 10 is the longest par 3 (at 220 yards) and has a massive green, with a clear-water-filled quarry and limestone cliffs to the right. The 15th (153 yards) sits back up against the ocean again. The wind can make my club choice swing anywhere from a five- to a seven-iron."

As alluded to above, part of the pleasure of playing El Camaleón is the relaxed setting at the Mayakoba resort, in Playa del Carmen. "The resort is very well done," Fred added. "There are a number of wonderful pools for the kids, a nice spa, and a beautiful beach. There's everything you could hope for to make it a nice experience for the family." If you've made it this far to tee it up at El Camaleón, you owe it to yourself to visit the ruins at Tulum or Chichén Itzá, which provide an illuminating window into Mayan life a thousand years ago.

FRED FUNK has been a professional golfer since 1981 and joined the PGA Tour in 1989. He's thus far notched eight victories on tour, including: 1992 Shell Houston Open; 1995 Ideon Classic at Pleasant Valley–Buick Challenge; 1996 B.C. Open; 1998 Deposit Guaranty Golf Classic; 2004 Southern Farm Bureau Classic; 2005 The Players Championship; and 2007 Mayakoba Golf Classic. Always a contender, Fred ranks sixteenth in career earnings on the PGA Tour. A native of Maryland and a graduate of the University of Maryland, Fred now lives in Florida with his wife and three children.

If You Go

▶ **Getting There:** El Camaleón is forty-two miles south of Cancún, Mexico's Yucatán Peninsula. Cancún is served by most major carriers.

▶ **Course Information:** El Camaleón (+52 984 206-3088) plays 7,024 yards from the tourney tees to a par 72; it has a slope rating of 137. Green fees range from $165 to $238. Please note: The course is closed in the two weeks preceding the Mayakoba Golf Classic.

▶ **Accommodations:** The Fairmont Mayakoba (800 441 1414; www.fairmont.com/mayakoba) has 401 rooms overlooking either the beach or the adjacent jungles.

BAY HARBOR AND BEYOND

RECOMMENDED BY **Brandon Tucker**

There's a certain pleasure in hitting off from an elevated tee. First, there's the vista that allows you to transcend any anxieties concerning the hole or round of golf at hand and embrace the larger world—and remind you of your relatively small place therein. Second, there are the obvious benefits of gravity—you can mentally scratch thirty or forty yards off the scorecard yardage from your perch above the fairway, and rest assured that if you happen to hit it a little low, you'll still make it to the short stuff . . . or at least over the junk. Finally, there's the joy of watching the ball soar into the sky, hang there, and slowly make its way to terra firma. It may be the closest many of us come to the sensation of unassisted flight!

"If there's a signature shot of northern Michigan golf, it's the elevated tee-off," Brandon Tucker began. "Whether you're at Treetops in Gaylord, over at Bay Harbor in Boyne County, or up at Timberstone on the Upper Peninsula, you'll find a number of spectacular elevated tees. I think that Robert Trent Jones, Sr. minted the northern Michigan notion of this style of hole with the 6th on the Masterpiece Course at Treetops—a steeply sloped par 3. I grew up playing competitive golf in suburban Detroit, and was blown away when I first visited the northern part of the state to compete—the scenery and elevation changes were so dramatic. When I play these courses with fellow golf writers, it's great fun to watch their emotions. They seem equally impressed."

For residents on either coast who may think of Ireland or Hilton Head or Bandon Dunes when the notion of a golf escape surfaces, northern Michigan does not generally make the short list for consideration—if it makes the list at all. This is an oversight that should be rectified. For starters, there is a plethora of golf courses open to the public in the region—twenty-plus in the Petoskey–Harbor Springs–Boyne City area, and another

dozen just south around the town of Gaylord. The north woods setting is both beautiful and nostalgic, replete with small towns that have largely resisted the homogenizing influence of the big chains and a smattering of luxurious old-style resorts that recall the good life of a bygone era. Some of the tracks offer Lake Michigan views, further augmenting their appeal. There's great sailing and fishing in the lake and surrounding rivers for those who wish to supplement their greenside leisure activities. Perhaps best of all, northern Michigan is still a golf travel bargain, with many packages available to lure players to the heartland. "The experience is not overly ritzy—with the exception of the properties at Bay Harbor," Brandon continued. "The tone of the region is understated, but the value is exceptional. If you're like me and want nonstop golf on a golf-oriented trip, visit in the summer. It's light from 5 A.M. to 10 P.M., so fifty-four holes are very conceivable—even with a few breaks in between!"

Pushing north from Detroit (or east from Traverse City, which also has commercial air service), you'll first reach Treetops. This resort in Gaylord is home to four par 72 layouts—the Masterpiece (by Robert Trent Jones, Sr.), the Premier (by Tom Fazio), the Signature (by Rick Smith, who's better known for his golf instruction), and the Tradition (also by Smith). Treetops is also home to a pleasing novelty—the nine-hole Threetops, widely considered the best par 3 course in the country. Threetops has historically hosted the Par 3 Shootout, where a foursome of big-name pros gun for $540,000 in prize money—plus a million-dollar bonus for a hole-in-one. (Lee Trevino walked away with a cool million in 2001 after acing the 137-yard 7th hole.) The Masterpiece was the first course at Treetops, and remains the resort's most sought-after track. While it may not have the thirteen elevated tees (by Brandon's count) that you'll find at Signature, it has the aforementioned 6th hole—the par 3 that plays 180 yards from the back tee and drops 120 feet to a well-bunkered green. The vantage point from the 6th tee is said to have inspired the name "Treetops." You'll enjoy more excellent vistas of this densely forested property—a mélange of oaks, maples, beeches, pines, and hemlocks—from the 15th tee, which rests seventy-five feet above the fairway, and plays to short par 4.

Bay Harbor is the gem of greater Petoskey, and, for many Michiganders, of all the North Country courses. It's one of the crowning achievements of Arthur Hills, a prolific Ohio-based designer who has nearly 200 new courses and 120 renovations to his credit. Bay Harbor's story mirrors that of its slightly more famous neighbor across the lake, Whistling Straits. The property was once a large cement operation, with limestone and

OPPOSITE:
The Links nine at Bay Harbor wanders along the shores of Lake Michigan.

DESTINATION

29

shale quarries and towering kilns. Petoskey Portland Cement ceased operations in 1983, and its unsightly remnants sat on scenic Little Traverse Bay for a decade until plans were drawn up for a luxury development. Work on the twenty-seven-hole layout, which moves amidst lakeside bluffs, unblemished woodlands (adjacent to the plant), and a shale quarry, soon began. In 1996, the Links, the Preserve, and the Quarry opened to great acclaim. The Links layout meanders 150 feet above Lake Michigan, making for some awe-inspiring views, and the Preserve is a standout woodland track. But it's the Quarry that steals the show for most visitors. (Quarries of a certain size seem to provide an inspiring palette for the adventurous architect—see Chambers Bay on page 219.) This track skirts an abandoned shale quarry. Forty-foot walls of black rock stand in sharp contrast to emerald fairways—the imagery the Quarry offers is almost exhilarating enough for you to forgive the many forced carries that it calls for. The two par 5s here are standouts. The first, 561-yard number 3, beguiles you from the fairway with long views of Lake Michigan before asking you to fly a portion of the quarry to the green below. Number 5 is shorter, but requires a water carry off the tee and then again on your approach—though the green's backdrop, sheer shale walls punctuated by a natural waterfall, will make your shot to the green sweet, even if it's coming on your fifth of sixth stroke.

Brandon still happily recalls his first experience with northern Michigan's glorious downhill tee shots. "I was fourteen or fifteen, and playing my first practice round at the Fazio course (Premier) at Treetops; at this point in my life, I had no idea who Tom Fazio was. It was pouring down rain, and my dad and I had the whole course to ourselves. Down around Detroit, you're used to hearing freeway noise wherever you play. It was so quiet here. I remember coming to the 4th hole—the first par 3 on the course—and looking straight down this steep hill to the green. I had never seen a hole like this before. I teed off with a short-iron (the hole is only 143 yards from the blues) and the ball went up and up and up. When it finally landed—about six feet from the hole—it made a ball mark the size of a grapefruit."

BRANDON TUCKER is a staff writer and editor for WorldGolf.com, where he's responsible for GolfEurope.com, MichiganGolf.com, and other regional sites and also blogs regularly. While Brandon was based in Europe, his travels took him to golf courses in Scotland, Ireland, England, Wales, Germany, Portugal, Poland, and the Czech Republic. A competitive golfer since the age of ten, Tucker is a product of Ann Arbor Huron High School

DESTINATION 29

in Michigan, where in 1999 he cocaptained his D1 state finalist golf team. Brandon received a bachelor's degree from the Indiana University School of Journalism, with a minor in music. In the two years after college, he served as a reporter and photographer for WTXL, an ABC News affiliate in Tallahassee, Florida. He then left to become producer of onboard television for Norwegian Cruise Lines, serving on ships in Alaska, the Caribbean, and Central America. Though he's played across Europe, beautiful northern Michigan is still his favorite spot to tee it up.

If You Go

▶ **Getting There:** Gaylord (home of Treetops) is a roughly four-hour drive from Detroit, which is served by most major carriers; Petoskey and Bay Harbor are another hour up the road. Traverse City, which is just an hour from your northern Michigan golf hubs, is also served by a number of carriers, including American (800-433-7300; www.aa.com), United (800-864-8331; www.united.com), and Northwest (800-225-2525; www.nwa.com).

▶ **Course Information:** The Masterpiece at Treetops plays 7,007 yards from the black tees to a par 71; it has a slope rating of 141. The Premier plays 6,832 yards from the tips to a par 72; it has a slope rating of 134. The Signature plays 6,653 yards from the blacks to a par 70; it has a slope rating of 136. Green fees at Treetops (888-TREETOPS; www.treetops.com) vary from $65 to $125, depending on the course and the season. The most popular combination at Bay Harbor (Quarry/Links 18) plays 6,724 yards from the tips to a par 70 (it's a par 72 layout from other tees); it has a slope rating of 145. Green fees at Bay Harbor range from $79 to $199.

▶ **Accommodations:** Treetops/Sylvan Resort (888-TREETOPS; www.treetops.com) in Gaylord has 254 deluxe rooms to complement its eighty-one holes of golf. Close to Bay Harbor, there's the upscale Inn at Bay Harbor (800-462-6963; www.innatbayharbor.com) and Harbor Resort & Marina. (231-439-2400; www.bayharbor.com). The Petoskey Area Visitors Bureau (800-845-2828; www.boynecountry.com) provides an overview of lodging options in the region.

ALGONQUIN GOLF CLUB

RECOMMENDED BY **Thomas McBroom**

It must be a bit of a mixed blessing for a golf course architect to be called in to undo the work of one of his/her peers. No matter the rationale for the redesign, you can't help but think that your presence on the site is somehow an indictment of your precursor's work—that it didn't make the grade, and you're there to make it better.

The task must be all the more daunting when the course you've been asked to reimagine was the handiwork of Donald Ross. But Thomas McBroom was up to the challenge.

"When Fairmont became involved with the Algonquin Resort, they wanted to make it an international golf destination," Tom began. "The existing course wasn't going to cut it on this level—it was too short, and deficient in a number of other respects, though it was blessed with a fine location. I had some misgivings about tinkering with a Ross design, and contacted the Donald Ross Society to see if they had any historical records about the layout—and any thoughts that might come to bear on how the course should be reworked to honor Ross's design. They gave me the go-ahead to proceed as I deemed fit. This was one of Ross's 'mail order' courses—he did the routing on paper, but never visited the site, hence the course did not really benefit from the full expertise of the master."

The Fairmont Algonquin is in the hamlet of St. Andrews by the Sea at the southern tip of New Brunswick, the Canadian province that may be best known for its Atlantic salmon. The town was settled in 1783 by Empire loyalists, residents of the thirteen English colonies who did not want to be associated with the newly minted United States after England's defeat in the Revolutionary War. Many of the town's buildings date back to the late 1700s; some were floated intact on barges across Passamoquoddy Bay from the soon-to-become-state of Maine. St. Andrews by the Sea takes its name from a little golfing town

OPPOSITE:
Algonquin
abuts both
Passamoquoddy
Bay and the
Bay of Fundy,
and the back
nine offers
a feast of
ocean vistas.

DESTINATION

30

135

in Scotland—"The course connects to town just like the Old Course connects to the other St. Andrews," Tom pointed out. "I was as captivated by the town and its rich history as I was by the course's potential." Like the town, the Algonquin was established by Americans; the venerable Tudor-style hotel opened its doors in 1889 and the first course, a nine-holer (essentially a pitch-and-putt), was laid out in 1894. (Canadian Pacific Railway, which is responsible for many great hotels, bought the property in 1903, and later commissioned Ross's work.)

With the blessing of the Donald Ross Society and the backing of Fairmont, Tom and his team set out to create the new Algonquin. "We began with the premise of connecting the course to the ocean and finding a better site for the clubhouse," Tom continued. "We were able to buy a fifty-acre parcel of land to the west, which allowed us to add a few more oceanfront holes and relocate the clubhouse to a spot that would have an ocean view. Looking at the existing layout didn't hamper our vision of what the new course could be. We basically rebuilt the course with all-new routing to make the most of the land.

"Though we took out the original course, I was sensitive to the fact that the original work on Ross's design had been done the old-fashioned way—that is, without moving much earth. And that's what we tried to do. We already had beautiful rumpled terrain that cozied up to the sea, and there was no need to reinvent the landscape. It ebbs and flows with its natural contours; greens would rise up from existing landforms; fairways would lie as they do, pushing up the bunkering. I've heard a number of people say that the course appears quite old. I take that as a great compliment."

The front nine at Algonquin unfolds over much of the territory that comprised the original layout, wandering near the edge of the town. (A keen eye may be able to spot a few of the old tee boxes among the fescue.) Regulars feel that the thickly wooded front is a bit more demanding than the back and appeals to shot makers. This may be most evident on the 6th, a slightly uphill 373-yard par 4. The tactic for your tee shot seems obvious, but is much more nuanced. Play a bold drive to the left side of the fairway, and you risk leaving yourself in a deep bunker there—though if you clear it, you'll have an easy wedge to the green. Play tentatively to the right and you take the chance of leaking into the woods that eat into the fairway at the 200-yard mark.

If the front is for shot makers, the back nine is for everyone else. Here, Algonquin marches toward the Bay of Fundy, the body of water that separates northern Maine and southern New Brunswick from the island of Nova Scotia. Now your golf shots are framed by yachtsmen's spinnakers and lobstermen plying their trade. The par 4 11th brings you to the edge of the water with a green that seems to be suspended over the sea. The par 3 12th is an ode to the 7th at Pebble Beach, though it plays a bit longer at 156 yards. The short par 5 13th continues your coastal odyssey. The fairway bends with the contours of the cliffs, and your approach to the green is framed by the town of St. Andrews by the Sea. More remnants of the old Algonquin lurk as you make your way to the end of your round. The original clubhouse—one of Canada's oldest standing clubhouses—rests near the 17th green, a reminder of the many rounds played here over the last century.

THOMAS McBROOM is a golf course architect hailing from Toronto whose designs combine an understanding of and fascination with the history and tradition of the game combined with his own unique creative flair and vision. An architect since 1988, Tom has won scores of awards for his designs; in 2006, twelve of his designs were included in *SCOREGolf* magazine's list of Canada's top 100 courses, more than any other living architect. These include Beacon Hall, Crowbush Cove, Rocky Crest, Deerhurst Highlands, Le Géant, Deer Ridge, Bell Bay, Heron Point, Granite Golf, Algonquin, Lake Joseph, and National Pines. His recent design in Kamloops, British Columbia—Tobiano—was named Canada's best new course in 2008 by *SCOREGolf.*

DESTINATION

30

If You Go

▶ **Getting There:** St. Andrews by the Sea is roughly one-and-a-half hours from St. John, New Brunswick's largest city. St. John is served by Air Canada (888-247-2262; www.air-canada.com), with connections from Montreal, Toronto, and Halifax.

▶ **Course Information:** Algonquin Golf Club (506-529-8165; www.fairmont.com/algonquin) plays 6,908 yards from the back tees to a par 72; it has a slope rating of 134. Green fees range from $49 to $99 CAD. The course is open May to October.

▶ **Accommodations:** The Algonquin (866-540-4403; www.fairmont.com/algonquin), with 234 rooms, is considered New Brunswick's most elegant seaside hotel.

BLACK MESA GOLF CLUB

RECOMMENDED BY **Baxter Spann**

There are desert courses that demand precision shots from sliver of green to sliver of green, lest your ball perish in the saguaro. There are Old World links with their unruly fescue-laden hummocks and blind tee and approach shots.

And then there's Black Mesa—a track north of Sante Fe, New Mexico, that might be construed as a hybrid of the two.

"I've been designing courses since 1979, and this was the most interesting and spectacular site I have ever had the opportunity to work with," Baxter Spann said. "We had 1,500 acres, and the possibilities were overwhelming at first. The combination of on-site landforms and off-site views is second to none. The first time I saw it, the summer rains had been through, and the native grasses were in green vigor, with seedheads blowing in the wind. It was a surreal experience to see property in the middle of New Mexico mesa country with dune-like formations like you'd see on the Irish coast."

Black Mesa Golf Club sits in the middle of a swatch of badlands/canyon terrain where one half-expects to find bandits lurking in the shadows and wild horses feeding on the hearty grasses that somehow find enough moisture here to survive. The course rests well above the surrounding high desert plains, offering sweeping views of the Sangre de Cristo mountains to the east; Los Alamos, home of the Manhattan Project (which led to the creation of the atomic bomb), is a dozen miles to the west. "One of the great experiences in arriving at this property to me was always the sequence of driving through the gate, through the cottonwoods along the old irrigation ditch, and up the rolling slopes to the high ground at the windmill, where the clubhouse now stands," Baxter continued. "The road covers about a mile from the point where you leave the paved road until you reach the windmill. In this distance, you have a chance to be absorbed into the site, and

OPPOSITE:
New Mexico canyons meet rolling links-like land at Black Mesa, a different take on dry-country golf.

DESTINATION

31

totally leave behind thoughts of the day-to-day world." The routing rambles up and down and around the canyons, with Black Mesa itself—a monolithic volcanic outcropping—looming at the southern edge of the course. Stark sandstone foothills and natural ridges line the fairways, suggesting Palm Desert or Tucson; but instead of forced carries over cactus and arroyos, the undulating fairways frequently allow bump-and-run shots to greens resting in box canyons. "I think that one of the factors that make a course truly stand out is how well it evinces its surroundings," Baxter ventured. "We were very conscious of this with the design at Black Mesa, trying to celebrate the surroundings and weave the course into the fabric of northern New Mexico."

The relatively short (339 yards from the blues) 1st hole at Black Mesa sets the stage for what's to come. Canyon walls frame the left, right, and rear of the field of play. Waste bunkers skulk in the foreground, more traditional bunkers wait in the distance; wild grasses flutter to the left, lining a ravine. The green is tucked at the base of the hills to the left. There's a fairway out there—a fairly generous one—but you won't see much of it from the tee. Locals know to select one of the bunkers as an aiming point; you can cut more off the hole by trying to carry the ravine, though the benefits of such a risky play are dubious. As you make your way to the fairway, a notch in a hill behind the green exposes the valley below and the Sangre de Cristos in the distance.

"I played Tobacco Road (a Mike Strantz design) near Pinehurst when we were designing Black Mesa," Baxter continued. There are a number of wild strategic holes there. On the 1st hole, you play through two dramatic mounds—visually it intimidates the heck out of you, but when you get out there, you see that the fairway is nearly 100 yards wide. Seeing this course freed me up to do Black Mesa. Some people who play the course come away feeling it's tricked up; I've heard this comment often. I think many American golfers have been conditioned to play 'cart golf,' riding along the paths of very formulaic parkland golf courses. They've never had the chance to play in Scotland or Ireland. We knew that Black Mesa would blow some people's minds, but I think that people with a spirit of adventure and variety will appreciate it. I think it says something about the track that many players who don't enjoy it the first time grow to like it the next time around. It's not a card-and-pencil kind of course [to paraphrase Alister Mackenzie]. It's more of a match-play course, where you play each hole for what it is."

The dune-laden coast of Ireland and the rugged canyon country of northern New Mexico have both been shaped in part by the wind. Very light people or those prone to wearing loose, billowing clothing, beware—this is the kind of wind that can carry you away! "I've been out there when the winds have gusted to sixty or seventy miles per hour," Baxter said. "And you can't simply say that prevailing winds are from one direction. In the morning it tends to come out of the north; in the afternoon, hard out of the southwest." Beyond causing chapped lips, the wind particularly comes to bear on Black Mesa's short par 4s. Baxter's favorite is number 14, which plays slightly uphill toward a large natural mound that rests in the center of the fairway. "The fairway is 100 yards wide, but you have some interesting choices to make off the tee," he described. "Long hitters can try to fly the mound, but if you wander left, you'll find the largest bunker complex on the course. The safest shot off the tee is behind the mound—but then you're behind the mound, making for a blind approach."

BAXTER SPANN is vice president of Finger Dye Spann, Inc., where he's been part of the design team since 1979. His work includes master planning for golf course/residential developments and numerous remodeling projects, as well as dealing with environmental issues relating to golf course development. He holds a Bachelor of Landscape Architecture degree from Louisiana State University and is a registered landscape architect in the states of Texas and Louisiana and a member of the American Society of Landscape Architects. Baxter's original designs include Sycamore Ridge Golf Course in Spring Hill, Kansas, and Marty Sanchez Links de Santa Fe in New Mexico; his renovations include Memorial Park Golf Course in Houston and Beaumont Country Club in Beaumont, Texas.

If You Go

▶ **Getting There:** Black Mesa is in the town of La Mesilla, roughly forty minutes north of Santa Fe and one-and-a-half hours north of Albuquerque. Albuquerque has service from most major carriers.

▶ **Course Information:** Black Mesa (505-747-8946 www.blackmesagolf.com) plays 7,307 yards from the black tees to a par 72; it has a slope rating of 141. Green fees range from $62 to $67.

▶ **Accommodations:** The Santa Fe Visitors and Convention Bureau (800-777-2489; www.santafe.org) lists the broad variety of accommodations available.

MONTAUK DOWNS

RECOMMENDED BY **Damon Hack**

If the United States has an equivalent to the springy turflands of Fife, it is found toward the tip of Long Island, New York. Here you come upon the sandy soil and tree-growth-stunting winds that mark the eastern coast of Scotland. And here you find the first great flowering of American golf. Long Island was not the site of the nation's first golf course, nor its first eighteen-hole layout, but it is the home of the country's first *great* golf course: the National Golf Links of America, C.B. MacDonald's paean to his favorite holes from the courses he'd visited in Scotland. Other giants followed—William Flynn's Shinnecock Hills (on land adjoining the National, both in Southampton), and Willie Park's Maidstone (in Easthampton), to name a couple. For most of us, an outing at the National, Shinnecock, or Maidstone qualifies as a once-in-a-lifetime event—after all, entree to these courses is more guarded than the sanctums of many heads of state.

Fortunately, Long Island has also long been a sanctuary of quality *public* golf. One of the early public links was Salisbury Links, established in 1918 by Joseph J. Lannin, proprietor of the Garden City Hotel, after a course of the same name went private and changed its name to Cherry Valley. (Salisbury Links is now a three-course complex called Eisenhower Park.) Anyone who follows professional golf has likely heard of Bethpage Black, one of five public courses at Bethpage State Park in Farmingdale, and a regular U.S. Open stop. Fewer have heard of Montauk Downs—though that might change.

"My wife has some friends out in the Hamptons, and we started heading out to visit them around 2000 or 2001," Damon Hack recalled. "Being a golfer, I was looking for a place to play while everyone else was hanging out. Bethpage was preparing to host the 2002 U.S. Open at the time, and there was a lot of talk about the renaissance in public golf—the Bethpage event was being called 'The People's Open.' It was in this context that

OPPOSITE:
Though it is situated at the tip of Long Island amidst America's best links land, Montauk Downs has more of a parkland feel—though the winds can certainly come into play.

DESTINATION

32

143

I first heard about Montauk Downs. After playing there just one time, I could remember the routing very clearly. I generally don't recall each of my shots during a round, but when I play at Montauk, they stick with me. The routing is that special."

Like so many golf courses, Montauk Downs was initially created as part of larger real estate venture, commissioned by an entrepreneur named Carl Fisher. Among his many ventures (which included the Indianapolis Speedway and the establishment of Miami Beach as a resort destination), Fisher staked out Montauk as the "Miami Beach of the North." He engaged Captain H.C.C. Tippet to draw up the plans; it's well known that Tippet was assisted by C.B. MacDonald, though MacDonald took no credit for the design. The course, which opened in 1927, was augmented by a first-rate clubhouse designed by Stanford White; green fees were $2.50 during the week and $3.50 on weekends. Montauk wanders through hilly, wooded terrain and around ponds and lakes; though more a parkland layout than a links, Montauk Downs is subject to the vagaries of links-like conditions. "You get days when there's no wind, days with heavy wind, days when the wind is constantly switching around," Damon said. "It makes things fun—and challenging."

Montauk Downs' initial Roaring Twenties glory was short lived. Black Tuesday ruined its owner, and over the next three decades the course slowly fell into disrepair. By the 1960s it was a shadow of itself, and its new owner—the Bank of Israel—retained Robert Trent Jones, Sr. to reinvigorate the course. Working with his sons (Robert, Jr. and Rees) at his side, the elder Jones conducted a significant redesign, resulting in the course visitors see today. As of this writing, Montauk is in the final stages of another upgrade, overseen by Rees Jones; Jones donated his services, as the budgets didn't allow for a designer of his caliber. His motivations for doing so: fond memories of working alongside his father, and a belief that the future of golf rests in public facilities.

"One of the benefits of Montauk Downs is that it is at least two-and-a-half hours from New York City," Damon continued. "Because of the distance, it doesn't get the traffic that Bethpage Black gets. I can't say that Montauk is as grand as Bethpage Black, but it's every bit as memorable. The strength of its design and the variety make it stand out. I don't love it because I can tear it up, but because it has the potential to tear me up."

The signature hole at Montauk Downs is the par 3 12th, which plays across a ravine, often into the wind. But Damon's fondest memory comes from the 13th hole, a par 5 dogleg left. "It was a gorgeous summer day in the middle of the week, not a cloud in the sky, and I was playing by myself," he recalled. "The 13th has an elevated tee and runs downhill; if you hit a good drive, it's possible to go for the green in two—even if you're just a mid-handicapper. I caught my drive pretty good, and when I reached my ball, I felt like I could maybe make it. I was so caught up in the moment—the beautiful day, the solitude, the good drive I'd hit—that I called my best friend in Los Angeles. I got his voicemail, and left a message that began like this: 'I'm on the 13th at Montauk, I just killed a drive, and I'm debating between a 4-iron and 5-wood to go for the green. I think I'm going to hit the 5-wood.' I put the phone down near the ball and hit, then picked it up. 'Buddy, I'm left of the green,' I said, 'but I should still make par.' My friend and I still talk about that phone message. I was so elated, and wanted to share the moment with a good friend who loves the game as much as I do, and can appreciate how I love this course."

DAMON HACK is a senior writer for *Sports Illustrated*, covering the PGA Tour and the National Football League. He formerly worked at *The New York Times*, where he covered golf and football, *Newsday*, where he covered golf and football, and *The Sacramento Bee*, where he covered just about everything. Damon prefers golf at sunset, anything pertaining to UCLA, and the magic of the changing of the seasons in the northeast. He dreams of breaking 80 before he checks out of this big, blue marble.

If You Go

► **Getting There:** Montauk is approximately 130 miles from Manhattan, at the eastern tip of Long Island—which could be anywhere from a two-and-a-half to a five-hour drive, depending on traffic. Southwest Airlines (800-435-9792; www.southwest.com) and U.S. Airways Express (800-428-4322; www.usairways.com) offer service into Islip, roughly thirty miles out onto Long Island.

► **Course Information:** Montauk Downs (631-668-1234; www.montaukdowns.org) plays 6,874 yards from the black tees to a par 72; its slope rating is 141. Green fees range from $36 to $82.

► **Accommodations:** Montauk Online (www.montauk-online.com) lists the range of accommodations available at this popular beach community.

THE HILLS

RECOMMENDED BY **Sir Bob Charles**

Most would agree that when it comes to golf notoriety, the North Island of New Zealand has hogged the Kiwi spotlight. First, the North Island gave us Kauri Cliffs, near the top of the island, then Cape Kidnappers in the Hawke's Bay region in the southeast. Both have quickly emerged as must-visit venues for sojourning golfers, who in the past may have opted to leave the South Island to traveling trout fishermen.

Jewelry mogul Michael Hill set out to change that, and his efforts attracted the attention of the man whom many consider to be the ambassador of New Zealand golf—British Open winner Sir Bob Charles. "Michael loves the game of golf, and owns some 500 acres just outside Arrowtown, on the South Island," Sir Bob described. "He had a little pitch-and-putt in his backyard, with three greens that you could play from different angles so you could take it to nine holes. Michael wanted to put the land to good use, and eventually decided that it should hold a golf course. He hired John Darby, a golf course architect and resort planner based in nearby Queenstown, to design The Hills. No expense was spared. I have a cottage nearby and visit the area regularly. After I had a chance to play, I realized the potential the course had to be a tournament venue—from a viewing aspect, it's one of the finest layouts I'd ever seen. The playing field is in a natural amphitheatre. There are courses like TPC Sawgrass that are built specifically to host spectators. The spectator aspect of The Hills is purely natural." With Sir Bob's encouragement, Michael Hill and John Darby added some finishing touches to The Hills; as a result, the course has hosted the New Zealand Open three years running, from 2007 to 2009. Few courses have been home to such a prestigious event in their first year of official operation.

Peter Jackson's *Lord of the Rings* trilogy showed the world what most Kiwis already knew—that the southwestern portion of the southern island of New Zealand is an area of

OPPOSITE:
The Hills is marked by rugged schist formations and vistas of surrounding mountains.

DESTINATION

33

147

incomparable natural beauty. The combination of steep mountains, dark green forests, snow-capped peaks, foaming waterfalls, and fingers of blue fiords make the region—known broadly as Fiordland—one of the most visually stunning temperate areas in the world. Arrowtown is just east of Fiordland, and enjoys a drier climate. "Arrowtown got its start in the 1860s when gold was discovered in the river," Sir Bob said. "It's surrounded by mountains; I can see three different ski fields from my cottage, all less than an hour away. Between the hiking, fly-fishing, hunting, skiing, and golf, it's one of New Zealand's premier resort areas."

While a majority of New Zealand's golf courses and golfers reside on the North Island, the game has its roots in the deep south, in the province of Otago. New Zealand's first club was established here in the city of Dunedin in 1871 by a Scotsman named Charles Ritchie Howden; indeed, it was the first club in the Southern Hemisphere. Initially called the Dunedin Golf Club, it's now known as the Otago Golf Club, and its Balmacewen Course is one of the jewels of Kiwi golf—on either island.

The setting that makes The Hills a great spectator course also makes it a memorable playing experience. Laid out on the site of a former deer farm, the course is encircled by the Remarkables mountains and the Crown Range, which include peaks approaching 8,000 and 6,000 feet respectively; guests are often treated to the play of snow-dusted peaks against the gray schist that dominates the site. The rugged schist formations that give The Hills its dramatic topography also lend it an almost masculine characteristic, a facet of the course's persona that reverberates in the many intrepid lines presented from the tee boxes that beg big hitters to push to their limits for scoring advantage. The Hills' aesthetics are softened by the presence of more than 50,000 red and silver tussock plants, which sway in a mesmerizing fashion when the breezes blow through the hills. The palette is finished off with ten ponds, all fed by Mill race (stream), which winds through the property.

"As the name suggests, The Hills is indeed quite hilly," Sir Bob continued. "In fact, on one hill in the middle of the course, you can see something like thirteen greens from one spot. I don't know of any other course in the world where this can be done. From a playing perspective, The Hills has a little bit of everything—driveable par 4s, reachable par 5s. There's great variety, and no two holes are alike. Overall it has a links atmosphere; there are trees on the perimeter of the playing areas, but they don't factor into your scoring. The 17th hole (called The Canyon) is The Hills' signature hole, a par 5 of 553 yards. On your tee shot, the first 300 yards of the fairway on the right are guarded by a large pond and a huge waste bunker; two bunkers lurk at the left edge of the landing area. Here the hole doglegs right; your second shot plays into a schist-faced canyon, where the fairway narrows as it approaches an undulating green."

SIR BOB CHARLES is widely regarded as New Zealand's greatest golfer. During his competitive career, he won more than seventy-five titles worldwide, including the 1963 British Open, where he beat American Phil Rodgers in a playoff. (This made him the first lefty to ever win a major tourney.) Known as one of the game's best putters, he triumphed five times on the U.S. PGA Tour and claimed eight titles on the European Tour. He also won four New Zealand Opens and three New Zealand PGA championships before embarking on a successful senior career that included the Senior British Open in 1989 and 1993. Sir Bob was made a member of the Order of the British Empire (OBE) by Queen Elizabeth in 1972 and advanced to Commander in the same Order in 1992. He became Sir Bob Charles in 1999 when made a Knight Companion of the New Zealand Order of Merit. Sir Bob is also a successful golf course designer, having contributed to the designs at Formosa Country Club (Aukland), Millbrook (Arrowtown), Clearwater (Christchurch), and Matarangi (Coromandel Peninsula). He is a member of the World Golf Hall of Fame.

If You Go

▶ **Getting There:** The Hills is in Arrowtown, fifteen minutes from the Queenstown International Airport. Air New Zealand (800-262-1234; www.airnewzealand.com) offers service to Queenstown via Auckland or Christchurch.

▶ **Course Information:** The Hills (+63 3 409 8290; www.thehills.co.nz) plays 7,243 yards from the tourney tees to a par 72. While The Hills is a private club, management endeavors to accommodate visitors whenever possible. Green fees for guests are $500 NZD (approximately $300 USD at the time of this writing).

▶ **Accommodations:** The Discover Arrowtown website (www.arrowtown.org.nz) highlights lodging options in the region.

PINEHURST NO. 2

RECOMMENDED BY **Tim Moraghan**

A recent mass-market advertisement for a major credit card company features a list of "things to do while you're alive." Among the items on the list, which includes "write a screenplay, swim in all five oceans, visit the Taj Majal, and see Iguaçu Falls," is a directive to "Play Pinehurst No. 2." This says a great deal about the public perception of this venerable course. For those who are only modestly acquainted with the game, Pinehurst No. 2 means a very special golf experience. Tim Moraghan echoes those sentiments—though from a very educated golf perspective.

OPPOSITE:
The challenge on
Pinehurst No. 2
really begins
when you get
near the green.

"For me, Pinehurst is the home of golf in the United States," Tim began. "There's all the early history, from James Walker Tufts's discovery of the sand hills to Donald Ross's time here. There's also all the modern-day history, with so many memorable tourneys held on Pinehurst No. 2. Pinehurst has everything you could want as a golf purist, and all you could want in a golf destination. There's such a laid-back feeling here, a perfect golf ambiance. As for No. 2, it's hard to put into words what makes it stand out. I say to friends, 'Play it a couple hundred times and tell me what makes it so special!' A good player will never get bored on that layout. And each time you play, you know everyone who has participated in the highest levels of the game of golf—from a player's perspective and an administrative perspective—has played it as well. You're in good company."

James Walker Tufts was a wealthy Bostonian who came south seeking a seasonal respite from the chilly winters of New England. When he came upon the mild climate, sandy, well-drained soil, and pine-scented air of eastern Carolina, Tufts knew he'd found his haven. He purchased 5,500 acres of land—considered of little value by local farmers—for $1 an acre, and hired landscape architect Frederick Law Olmsted (of New York's Central Park fame) to design a little village. The town he laid out stands mostly intact

DESTINATION

34

today. Golf came to Pinehurst in 1897, when Tufts and Dr. D. Leroy Culver, an amateur architect from New York, laid out the first nine holes of Pinehurst No. 1—at first, just 2,561 yards. The course had sand greens, and was described by the Pinehurst Outlook in 1898 as "Sixty acres of thoroughly cleared land, well fenced in and covered with a thick growth of rye, which will be kept short by a flock of more than 100 sheep." In 1899, the course was expanded to eighteen holes and 5,203 yards. Pinehurst No. 1's layout—and the general absence of snow in the eastern Carolinas—attracted golf aficionados from the north, including John D. Rockefeller and President William McKinley. When English golf legend Harry Vardon conducted a series of golf demonstrations at No. 1 in 1900, Pinehurst was on its way to being on the world golf map. And when Tufts convinced Scotsman Donald Ross to leave his first American gig in Boston and set up shop at Pinehurst that same year, the resort's future preeminence was assured.

Donald Ross had grown up playing golf in Royal Dornoch, and the sandhills around Pinehurst must have been reminiscent of his home. A fine player, Ross briefly held the course record at the original Pinehurst No. 1 with a score of 71; later he would redesign the course and sculpt three more courses at Pinehurst (Nos. 2, 3, and 4) and create designs for over four hundred more across North America—many of which he never visited. (For these so-called "mail-order" projects, Ross drew routings from topographical maps.)

Ross made liberal use of bunkers, both across the fairway and around the green. While players are often allowed a safe path to the green, they are generally punished for an overly aggressive approach.

Ross's architectural ethos is felt nearly everywhere golf is played in the New World, but his soul hovers closest to Pinehurst, where he lived and worked in a cottage behind the 3rd hole at No. 2, which was unquestionably his darling. Ross constantly tinkered with its design in the forty-one years between the course's opening in 1907 and his death in 1948. No. 2 doesn't have the majestic vistas and over-the-top aesthetic appeal of many of its perennial top ten course list companions. It doesn't even feel particularly daunting—until you've reached the first green. Eamon Lynch, managing editor of *Golf* magazine, summed it up nicely: "You can land a jumbo jet on the generous fairways without dislodging a pine-cone, but No. 2 is the toughest course on the planet from within fifty yards of the greens, which are tougher to hold than a nervous turkey on Thanksgiving. It takes only one chip shot rolling back to your feet to have confidence replaced by doubt and despair." Ron

Whitten, architecture editor of *Golf Digest*, has pointed out that while the greens at Pinehurst No. 2 are indeed challenging, they are quite different from the greens that Ross designed, which were more conventional. The extreme contours developed largely from methods of topdressing employed by early greenskeepers, which resulted in a height increase of over a foot, especially in the centers. "I always take the philosophy of hitting it in the middle of the green when I'm out on No. 2—the Nicklaus philosophy when playing the course," Tim added. "You play cute and hit for the pin, you can get in trouble—an easy par becomes a double bogey. I think a lot of the pros take a more aggressive approach— that's why you get one over or even par winning the U.S. Open."

Tim Moraghan has many fine memories from Pinehurst No. 2, both professionally and recreationally. Yet one of his most lasting remembrances comes from an encounter on the practice tee. "My dad was a wonderful player with a great short game," Tim recalled. "He was very proud of me when I got a job at Pinehurst (overseeing maintenance of No. 3), and came to visit. The first time we played No. 2 was Thanksgiving Day in 1980, a cold, crummy day. My dad played very well, scoring 80 or 81, though he was already in his mid-fifties. In 1994, he came to Pinehurst to see the U.S. Senior Open, which I was working on behalf of the USGA. By that time, he had cancer. As we were driving over to the course, he asked if Calvin Peete had qualified. You see, when my dad was little, he fell while ice skating and hurt his left elbow. It was permanently at a forty-five-degree angle, just like Calvin Peete's. At the practice range, we saw Calvin at the far end. My dad said, 'Just drop me off, I want to talk to him.' I dropped him off, but hung around. Pretty soon my dad was hitting balls with Calvin Peete, swapping stories about how best to hit balls with a crooked arm."

TIM MORAGHAN is president of Aspire Golf Consulting (www.aspiregolf.com), which provides a wide range of services covering all facets of the golf industry, including public, private, and resort golf courses, developers, golf course architects, club management, and, most important, golf course superintendents. Before launching Aspire, Tim was director of championships agronomy for the USGA. He has worked in the golf industry for over thirty years, from serving on grounds crews to constructing golf courses and working as a golf course superintendent. During his career, Tim also worked on professional events at the Tournament Players Club (Ponte Vedra) courses, Pinehurst Resort, and the Byron Nelson Classic at the Las Colinas Sports Club (Dallas). Tim has served as

DESTINATION

34

a rater for *Golf* magazine and *Golfweek*. Tim and his wife, Karen, founder and president of Hunter Public Relations (a golf and hospitality industry marketing consultancy) reside in Long Valley, New Jersey, and Hilton Head Island, South Carolina.

If You Go

▶ **Getting There:** The Pinehurst Resorts are in the southern Sandhills of North Carolina, approximately seventy-five miles from the Raleigh/Durham International Airport and 112 miles from the Charlotte International Airport. Both are served by most major carriers.

▶ **Course Information:** Pinehurst No. 2 (800-487-4653; www.pinehurst.com) measures 7,335 yards from the tourney tees and plays to a par 72; it has a slope rating of 137. Green fees are built around the many stay-and-play packages Pinehurst offers.

▶ **Accommodations:** There are three primary residences on the property—the Four Diamond, Holly, and Carolina hotels, and the slightly more everyman lodge, The Manor. For those playing No. 2, stay-and-play rates begin at $500 to $675 per night (including one round of golf), depending on when you visit.

DESTINATION

34

DEVIL'S PAINTBRUSH

RECOMMENDED BY **Mike Bell**

One of the potential boons of global warming may be that Canadian residents will be able to play more golf—even *more* golf. According to a study commissioned by the Royal Canadian Golf Society, 21.5 percent of Canada's citizenry played at least one round of golf in 2005, making Canada the highest per-capita golf-playing nation in the world. American golfers who like to think the game is *their* domain in the New World may take umbrage at the fact that golf has been played in Canada longer than it has in the United Sates, that the term "mulligan" is a Canadian invention, and that the phrase "You drive for show and you putt for dough" was coined by a Canadian. (Thanks to *ScoreGolf* editor Bob Weeks for compiling these tidbits.)

Hockey may be the national sport, but when the ice melts, Canadians are on the links.

Given the game's popularity and long pedigree, it should come as no surprise that Canada boasts a number of first-rate tracks, from mountain courses to seaside links to rugged minimalist designs on the plains. For pure density, variety, and quality, the greater Toronto area is hard to beat. As of this writing, there are 177 courses around Canada's economic capital, ranging from the city's five municipal courses to the venerable St. Georges. Two early-1990s additions to greater Toronto's impressive assemblage of courses are the Devil's Pulpit and Devil's Paintbrush courses, thirty-five miles north of the city proper in Caledon Village. The courses—joined under the umbrella of the Devil's Pulpit Golf Association—were the brainchild of Chris Haney and Scott Abbot, a couple of former journalists with an eye for minutiae who turned their interest in the arcane into a little board game called Trivial Pursuit. Using some of their newfound wealth, Haney and Abbot bought land on the Niagara Escarpment (a geologic formation spreading from

New York through Ontario, Michigan, Wisconsin, and Illinois, and most famously expressed in the cliff that forms Niagara Falls) and retained Dr. Michael Hurdzan and Dana Fry to design two courses. The former journalists' Midas touch continued—the two courses were named Canada's best new private venues in back-to-back years.

"I first played the Devil's Pulpit (Hurzdan's layout) in a tournament not long after it opened," recalled Mike Bell. "I fell in love with it. Pulpit is a very modern design, and though I'm a great fan of more traditional Stanley Thompson courses, I found its ground-breaking architecture intriguing. [More than 1.7 million cubic yards were moved to build Devil's Pulpit; as such, some have dubbed it an "earth sculpture."] I joined the club in 1998, and began playing Devil's Paintbrush (designed by Fry). The first few times I played it, I didn't quite know what to make of it. It's about as quirky and links-like as you can get without being on the coast of Scotland or Ireland. But it really grows on you. When I joined the club, I'd play eight times at Pulpit for each two times I'd play at Paintbrush. Now it's the opposite. The reason is simple: it's really fun to play."

As Mike noted, Devil's Paintbrush (named for a local wildflower, not the tool of a demonic designer) has all the facets of a links course—bold bunkers, billowing fescue in varying shades, blind shots, double greens, few trees, wild contours on both fairways and greens (and the occasional unexpected bounce), and beautiful stone walls lining the periphery of the playing area, made from stones found on the site. (Writing of the greens on GolfClubAtlas.com, Ran Morrissett noted "if you overanalyze them, you might go crazy. Just accept them as a crucial part of scoring well at the Paintbrush.") As for the water—well, Toronto and Lake Ontario are visible from the patio that adjoins Professor Rabbit's Hole—a traditional English pub that fittingly serves as the club's 19th hole. The eccentricity and charm of Devil's Paintbrush are best summed up in the 8th hole, a 574-yard par 5. Smack dab in the center of the fairway, about where the average player might land his/her drive, is the rock-wall foundation of a long-departed barn and an accompanying cattle drinking trough. The course notes point out that the hole is nearly as wide as it is long, so there's room to avoid the barn (though Mike pointed out that grass has been planted between the rocks of the foundation, and you can chip out if you're lucky). The right side poses a more expedient route, though here you must work your ball past what's believed to be the world's largest sod-walled bunker—sixty yards wide with walls as high as fifteen feet. At the green, there's a bunker on the front-left, pot bunkers on the front-right, and more trouble behind. "I've never seen anyone get there in two," Mike added.

OPPOSITE:
Devil's
Paintbrush
is beloved for
its eccentric
touches—
like the stone
foundation of an
old barn in the
middle of the
8th fairway.

DESTINATION

35

When Mike Bell thinks of Devil's Paintbrush, it's hard for him not to recall a friend whom he wanted to introduce to the course. "I spend part of each year in Thailand, and there I met a fellow named Chris Emms," Mike explained. "At first he was a client, but he became a close friend, and golf was a passion we both shared. Though he lived in Thailand, Chris was from the U.K., and on occasion we'd see each other there. On a visit a few winters back, he gave me a gift—a copy of *Fifty Places to Play Golf Before You Die*. I told him again about Devil's Paintbrush and said, 'You have to visit me in Canada and play, as this is one of those places you need to play before you die.'

"A few months later, I received a call from Chris's wife—he'd been diagnosed with a brain tumor, and was only given a few months to live. Chris never got a chance to play the Paintbrush. Every time I play it—or any course, for that matter—I think how golf is such a great way to make friendships. And that friendships are really what golf is all about."

MIKE BELL is founder and principal photographer of Photoscape (www.photoscape.ca), an international photography and publishing company whose clients include some of the finest golf and resort destinations in North America, Asia, and the Caribbean. Photoscape has published books featuring the historic golf courses of Stanley Thompson and, most recently, a commemorative book featuring the 2007 President's Cup for the members of the Royal Montreal Golf Club.

If You Go

▶ **Getting There:** Devil's Paintbrush is thirty-five miles north of Toronto, which is served by most major carriers, including Air Canada (888-247-2262; www.aircanada.com).

▶ **Course Information:** Devil's Paintbrush (905-584-0155; www.devilspulpit.com) plays 6,772 yards from the tips to a par 72. Though it is a private club, guests can sometimes find a game with the introduction of their local golf pro. Rates for guests are $95 to $140 CAD.

▶ **Accommodations:** The Toronto Convention and Visitors Association (800-499-2514; www.seetorontonow.com) lists the many lodging options available in Canada's largest city.

DESTINATION

35

BANDON TRAILS

RECOMMENDED BY **Grant Rogers**

When greeting-card-entrepreneur-turned-golf-course-developer Mike Keiser opened Bandon Dunes in 1998, more than a few people thought he was crazy. They were soon proved wrong: Bandon Dunes was immediately hailed as the seventh wonder of the golfing world. Its blend of a challenging links layout with jaw-dropping scenery and a low-key yet high-class ambiance has set a new standard in destination golf that has lived up to the resort's rather presumptuous slogan— "Golf as it was meant to be." When Tom Doak's Pacific Dunes was added to the mix in 2001, guests who'd come to play Bandon didn't wish to be diverted to the new track—that is, until they gave in to staff entreaties and played it. Soon, Pacific Dunes became the must-play course.

When Bandon Trails opened in 2005 and regular guests were encouraged to try it, there was much less resistance. After all, Mike Keiser's gambles had paid off handsomely twice before, and he'd retained one of the world's most celebrated architecture teams— Bill Coore and Ben Crenshaw—to craft the new course. Bandon's seaside real estate had been mostly used up, so the new course would have to be inland. Keiser had been taken with Sandhills Golf Club in Nebraska, where Coore and Crenshaw sculpted a monumental inland links course from immense dunes. He saw parallels between the Sandhills site and some undeveloped land at Bandon, south of the Bandon Dunes course. He let the architects loose, and what emerged was something wonderful, something that defies easy categorization.

"With Bandon Trails, Mike Keiser and his team have figured out a way to add eighteen more holes to the mix that are very different from the first two courses but that people really enjoy playing," Grant Rogers said. "I'm often asked, 'What does Trails remind you of?' I don't think of it vis-à-vis other courses, because any similarities end beyond a flicker

of similarity on one hole. It doesn't matter how good a player you are—on Trails, you have to play some cool shots to score well. I love playing courses where I know I'm going to use all my clubs, and on Trails, 14 doesn't seem like enough sometimes. Working at the resort, I hear a lot of discussions—well, elaborate and sometimes heated debates—about which of the three courses is better. It seems like Bandon Trails is holding its own in those debates, especially among those who've played it more than once."

Trails moves through a host of environments on its epic journey—epic in terms of both the grandeur of many of the holes and the amount of walking involved. (Even the more seasoned athletes will feel a bit of tightness in their calves as they climb the 18th fairway!) It begins on dunes land, moves into a rambling meadow, continues through a forest of Douglas firs and spruce, and concludes back in the dunes. Despite the absence of crashing surf, the scenery on Bandon Trails is every bit as inspired as its seaside brethren—the contrast of Coore and Crenshaw's gaping waste bunkers with towering conifers on this rolling terrain is both startling and exciting. While it is scenic, it's Trails' incredible playability that really makes it shine. "There are lots of elevated tees, and the ball really runs," Grant continued. "For a course that has so many trees, the driving is friendly. People like to see their ball go—it makes it fun.

"Your very first tee shot (on the 392-yard par 4 hole number 1) sets the tone for a round at Bandon Trails. It's a classic risk/reward drive, slightly uphill, through a saddle of sand dunes—you can cut off a lot of the hole if you can clear the big waste bunker on the left, though I like to play it to the right, as I know you can get a clear second shot from here with less chance of getting in trouble. The first green has one of the false fronts that you find on a lot of the holes at Trails. You need to give your approach some thought, so you're over the false front and on the putting surface. The 5th hole is one of my favorites anywhere, a real attention-getter. It's only 133 yards from the back tees, but it's a forced carry over a waste area with big traps in front and to the right—and you have no idea of the challenge of the green until you get there. If you're not on the same tier as the pin, a two-putt is a real accomplishment. I have more than once seen good players putt the ball off the green into one of the bunkers. I couldn't help but think that it was impressive to have a par 3 that was designed so even a good player could do that.

"I love to putt, and I'm very attracted to the greens at Trails. They're smooth and fast, and you have to use your imagination. They're different sizes and shapes, but the common denominator is that they're fun. I also really love the bunkering throughout the

OPPOSITE:
The par 3 17th shows all the facets of Bandon Trails: rolling terrain, towering fir trees, and, in the background, dunes.

DESTINATION

36

course. Some are so much fun to play out of, you almost look forward to the adventure of going in."

The treats go on and on. There's the narrow but drivable 8th that's lined with eleven bunkers, the long downhill par 4 11th with a lake that guards the approach (and seems to beckon even the most safely played shots to a watery death), the 242-yard par 3 12th that's uphill but open enough to let you run a low driver toward the pin. For Grant, it's the 14th that's his "can't wait to play" hole—a short and abruptly downhill par 4 (just 325 yards) with a tiny sliver of green with a steep drop-off on the left and bunkers on the right—that borders on ruthless. "It's little, but it's a classic," Grant added. "Everything is right there in front of you—you can see what you have to do to get to and hold the green, but it's one of the ultimate challenges to make it happen. It goes to show that you don't have to make a hole long to make it difficult." If there's ever a hole where fifty yards out can equal five strokes, this is it.

"I think that people tend to believe that they have more control over the golf ball than they actually do," Grant opined. "To me, golf is a good game to play to test out your luck. I think the walk overshadows the score, especially at a place like Trails. There are shots and situations you look forward to, but the walk should be your focus.

"I work with a lot of golfers here at Bandon, and I recall one occasion when a student wanted lots of technical tips—*lots* of technical tips! Once he ran out of questions, he asked me if there was anything else he could do to help ensure his success on the course. My response was, 'Enjoy the views.'"

GRANT ROGERS is director of instruction at Bandon Dunes, where he leads a team of PGA instructors in giving private lessons and oversees activities at the Bandon Dunes Golf Academy. Grant is among a very limited number of instructors who have reached Master Professional status; in 2007 he was recognized as "Teacher of the Year" for the Pacific Northwest section of the PGA. Grant enjoys helping people become better golfers; he also loves links golf, though proximity to the courses at Bandon Dunes has curtailed his once frequent adventures to Scotland and Ireland to play the classic links layouts.

▶ **Getting There:** Bandon Dunes Golf Resort is situated on the southern Oregon coast, approximately 250 miles from the Portland International Airport. While most visitors fly into Portland, there are commercial flights available into North Bend/Coos Bay, Oregon, twenty-five miles north of Bandon, which is served by United Airlines (800-864-8331; www.united.com).

▶ **Course Information:** Bandon Trails (800-742-0172; www.bandondunesgolf.com) plays 6,765 yards from the back tees, and plays to a par 71; it's slope rating is 132. Green fees for resort guests range from $75 in the winter season to $210 from May through October. Note that all the courses at Bandon are walking-only facilities.

▶ **Accommodations:** Bandon Dunes has a variety of understated but elegant lodging options available, from lodge rooms to cottages. Rates begin at $100 in the low season, $220 in the high season. Golf/lodging packages are available, especially in the off season. For a rundown of lodging options, visit www.bandondunesgolf.com or call 800-345-6008.

DESTINATION

36

OITAVOS DUNES

RECOMMENDED BY **Drew Rogers**

When Americans think of golf and Portugal—*if* they think of golf and Portugal—the Algarve region springs to mind. Portugal's answer to Spain's Costa del Sol, the Algarve lies on the country's extreme southern coast and boasts more than thirty courses, heavily patronized by Brits and other northern Europeans seeking a bit of sun to go with their golf (one might think of it as a less hurly-burly version of Myrtle Beach for the Old World).

The Lisbon area, 150 miles or so up the coast, presents a different—and perhaps slightly more refined—retreat. This capital city that dates back to the fifth century mixes remnants of its Moorish and Visigothic past with an energy that has spread through many of Europe's sleepier capitals in the last decade. A stroll to the hilltop Castelo de São George and through the labyrinthine streets of the Alfama district, with its painted tiles, fruit stands, and scent of cooking shellfish, is a feast for the senses. Its appeal is only enhanced by the nearby presence of a number of fine (and largely undersubscribed) golf courses—including Oitavos Dunes, just thirty minutes to the west of the city.

"I've played golf at great seaside venues all over the world," Drew Rogers began, "places where there's a great sense of tradition and a rich culture. Oitavos Dunes (and its accompanying resort, Quinta da Marinha) has this special sense of tradition, even though it's a relatively new course (built in 2001). This is thanks largely to the owners, the Champalimaud family, who are very eager to have visitors experience the best of what Portugal has to offer; in addition to the course, they've developed top-flight vineyards in the Douro and boast a world-class equestrian center. There's also the weather. Oitavos has a microclimate—it has weather patterns similar to San Diego, always temperate and sunny. It's a pleasing sea-side alternative to what you may experience in Great Britain."

OPPOSITE:
Oitavos Dunes offers sweeping views of the mountains of Sintra-Cascais National Park and the cliffs of Cabo de Roca, one of the westernmost points in continental Europe.

DESTINATION

37

Oitavos Dunes rests on high, rolling ground within the boundaries of Sintra-Cascais National Park, and offers unparalleled views of the park's mountains and the Atlantic below; its site a bit above the sea may contribute to its constantly pleasant temperatures. The course's dramatically rolling fairways run through a variety of terrains—sand dunes, stands of umbrella pines, rugged rock outcroppings, and back again to the dunes. Though not a pure links course, there are elements of links golf here. "It's a very open design, and the wind can really whip through," Drew continued. "Each time I walk or play the course, I come away with impressions of blue—the perennial blue sky, and the blue of the Atlantic that's in view on every hole. The links element of the course is especially pronounced on the dunes holes.

"Miguel Champalimaud (the course's owner) was very keen to keep the property as intact as possible, as it had been in the family for nearly ninety years. There's a tradition of land stewardship in the family—Miguel's grandfather planted many of the pines to help prevent erosion of the sand dunes. From a design perspective, there was great pressure to ensure that the golf coexisted with the elements of the land. Fortunately, the land had many fine natural features that lent themselves well to golf. We took the philosophy of moving as little earth as possible and using no more turf than necessary. The result is a rugged, natural golf layout—with sun!" (Oitavos Dunes was the first course in Europe to receive Audubon International's Certified Gold Audubon Signature Sanctuary designation, testament to Drew and Arthur Hill's success.)

It's not often that you find back-to-back par 3s on high-profile courses; this may be the results of the awesome precedent set by Alister MacKenzie at Cypress Point on the 15th and 16th holes. At Oitavos Dunes, Drew and Arthur Rogers rolled the dice on adjoining par 3s at 14 and 15, and they turned out to be Drew's favorite holes on the course. "The 14th plays 167 yards from an elevated tee to a green in a benched-in area of sand dunes," Drew described, "carrying over a draw of scrubby dunes. The cliffs of Cabo de Roca are in the background; the lighthouse out there is the westernmost point in continental Europe. There's a sense of nothingness beyond the green. Some days the wind howls in off the water and funnels past the green, enough to make this a hybrid or even a fairway wood shot. The hole does contour so you can run a low shot up. The 15th plays 186 yards back in the opposite direction, through a valley of dunes, to a long narrow two-tiered green that's nestled in an amphitheater of dunes. Where the wind is generally strong against you on the 14th, it helps you on the 15th." Golf travel expert Gordon Dalgleish has compared portions of the back nine at Oitavos Dunes to Cypress Point—high praise indeed.

"I can recall every time I've set foot on Oitavos Dunes, from walking the grounds before we'd broken ground to when the course hosted the Portugese Open," Drew reminisced. "Every time—from every vantage point—I've thought that there's no place I'd rather be at that moment, and that hopefully it will be like this next time I visit. It's a place to be experienced and appreciated and shared with others."

One of the appeals of a visit to Oitavos Dunes and the Atlantic coast near Lisbon is the chance to drink in the region's easygoing vibe. "The speed of life along the Estoril coast is very comfortable," Drew added. "People are very friendly and welcoming—tourism is their top industry, and they're conscious of this. The gastronomy is wonderful—great seafood and comfort foods, excellent wines from Douro and Alentejo (both reds and whites), and of course ports (tawny, vintage, and even white, a dry to semisweet aperitif). There are many things to do off the course between meals. One of Europe's best surfing beaches is nearby, and there are many walking and biking trails. The place has a healthy feel." Should time permit, the village of Sintra merits a visit; sequestered in the craggy mountains, it's home to a Moorish castle that has served as the summer residence of Portuguese royalty for 500 years.

If you've played Oitavos a few times and desire more golf, there are (as of this writing) nine other eighteen-hole tracks in the vicinity, including Troia Golf Championship Course, a classic Robert Trent Jones, Sr. design that's considered Portugal's toughest track.

DREW ROGERS is a principal and senior design partner in the golf architecture firm of Arthur Hills/Steve Forrest and Associates. A graduate of the University of Kentucky, he has been with the firm since 1992. His new designs include Legends Course at LPGA International (Daytona Beach), Mirasol Golf and Country Club (Palm Beach Gardens), Newport National Golf Club (Middletown, Rhode Island), Lowes Island Club—River Course (Potomac Falls, Virginia), The Club at Olde Stone (Bowling Green, Kentucky), and Oitavos Dunes. Drew's renovation projects include Chevy Chase Club (Chevy Chase, Maryland), Country Club of North Carolina (Pinehurst, North Carolina), Belle Haven Country Club (Alexandria, Virginia), Siwanoy Country Club (Bronxville, New York), University Club of Kentucky (Lexington, Kentucky), and Country Club of Columbus (Columbus, Georgia).

If You Go

▶ **Getting There:** Oitavos Dunes is in the seaside town of Cascais, about thirty minutes from Lisbon. Lisbon is served by many carriers, including Continental (800-525-0280; www.continental.com) and British Airways (800-247-9297; www.ba.com).

▶ **Course Information:** Oitavos Dunes (+351 21 486 0600; www.quintadamarinha-oitavosgolfe.pt) plays 6,893 yards from the championship tees to a par 71. Green fees are €115.

▶ **Accommodations:** Oitavos will soon have a five-star hotel—The Oitavos. In the interim, the Hotel Palacio (+351 21 545 8000; www.palacioestorilhotel.com) in nearby Estoril or the Hotel Albatroz in Cascais (+351 21 484 73 80; www.albatrozhotels.com) will more than suffice. If you prefer to stay right in the city, Visit Lisbon (+351 21 031 2700; www.visitlisboa.com) highlights the city's many lodging options.

DESTINATION

37

ROYAL DORNOCH

RECOMMENDED BY **Lorne Rubenstein**

Many visitors to Scotland—whether they have three days or three weeks—try to squeeze in as many courses as possible, moving from town to town and coast to coast to compress centuries of golf into a matter of hours. In the summer of 2000, Lorne Rubenstein took three months to focus on one town and one course (more or less).

"Back in 1977, I traveled from Canada to Great Britain to play in the British Amateur in England," Lorne began. "In preparation for the competition, I went to Dornoch, up in the Scottish Highlands. I'd read Herbert Warren Wind's article in *The New Yorker* about the course. Wind stated: 'It is the most natural course in the world. No golfer has completed his education until he has played and studied Royal Dornoch.' I was intending to go up for only a day or two, but I liked it so much, I stayed for a week. The place really imprinted itself on my brain. I started writing about the game soon after, and though I visited Scotland frequently to cover tournaments over the years, I had not been back to Dornoch . . . though the thought of going back always loomed in the back of my mind. In 2000, I decided to take a break from the tour to spend a summer there. It wasn't solely for the golf; I wanted to spend some time in a beautiful, quiet village in a remote place in Scotland. My wife is a college English teacher, so she was able to come along, as she didn't have classes in the summer."

Dornoch is roughly thirty miles north of Inverness, which some wags call Scotland's northernmost bastion of civilization. To put things in perspective, thirty miles north of Inverness places Dornoch at the same latitude as Hudson Bay and Juneau, Alaska; as such, many golf pilgrims never quite make it here. Written records show that golf has been played in Dornoch since at least 1616; only St. Andrews and Leith show records of earlier play. "People equate Scottish golf with the town of St. Andrews," Lorne has

observed, "but if you take the golf away, St. Andrews is still a charming university town with great historical significance. If you take the links away from Dornoch, it would be largely forgotten outside the town. If any town in the world deserves to be described as the village of golf, it's Dornoch."

The course that members and guests play today began to take shape in 1886 when Old Tom Morris was recruited from St. Andrews to add nine holes to the existing nine. Three years later another nine holes were added, and Dornoch was on its way to immortality. Donald Ross was a native of Dornoch, and played the course before and after Morris's additions. He was known to have spent long hours walking the course, and as greens-keeper here from 1895 to 1899, he made refinements to the design; the links here certainly informed his design work in America.

"Finding a place to live in town was difficult," Lorne continued, "as there just aren't many rentals available. Eventually I found a seedy flat above the only bookstore in town. But it had a view of an ancient cathedral, and I'm as much a bookstore aficionado as I am a fan of golf. Dornoch is one of the most arresting places I've visited, snuggled between the sea and the mountains. There's a lovely path above the golf course that you can walk. I also did a lot of cycling on the country roads. The chance to take in the larger landscape and get to know the people was just as important to me as gaining an understanding of the course." Some visitors to Scotland will comment on the reserve and reticence of the populace. For Lorne, time and familiarity melted away much of this reserve. "Dornochers are skeptical by nature of people who would like to bring their outside ways to the village, but they soon warm to you. You have to prove yourself, to show that you have come to Dornoch because you want to experience their way of life, not to transport yours there."

There are so many fine moments at Dornoch. The tee shot on the 161-yard par 3 6th (Whinny Brae), where any shot vaguely to the right slowly falls away into oblivion; the tee shot on the dogleg par 4 14th (Foxy), where a well-struck draw places you in the best position to approach the green. One of Lorne's favorite moments comes on the 3rd hole. "When you come around the corner from the 2nd green, you pass some hedges, and then the entire courses spreads itself out, all there for your viewing. It's golf on open ground with an ocean view. I knew it from my first visit in 1977, but it's still powerful to me.

"Many days I would play first thing in the morning with half a bag of clubs, and be done by nine; you don't need all fourteen clubs out there, as you can play so many inven-

OPPOSITE:
Golf has been
played around
Dornoch since
1616. Royal
Dornoch has the
distinction of
being laid out
(in part) by
Old Tom Morris
and maintained
(for a time) by
Donald Ross.

DESTINATION

38

tive shots on the ground. The rest of the day, I'd go for walks, bike rides, or spend a few hours in the bookstore. Sometimes in the afternoon I might go to the pub on the second floor of the golf club and watch players coming in while sipping a club ale or single malt. They even have wireless now in the pub, but that wasn't available during our summer, and I can't say I missed it. I might go back out on the course around nine in the evening. My wife doesn't play golf, but she'd often accompany me. I wouldn't necessarily play eighteen holes—I might play five or six, or just stop every now and then and hit a shot. Other times, I'd take a book and sit on a bench that's near the sixteenth green. Some evenings we'd walk out to the farthest reaches of the course, near the ninth tee. Out there, you feel like you're on the edge of the world. The short 13th became a favorite during my summer. I recall one night when the wind was blowing hard across the green from the sea, and I hit a variety of shots with different clubs—holding shots against the wind, riding the wind, hard hooks on the wind. I could have stayed there all evening, because there were so many ways to play the hole."

If you make it as far north as Royal Dornoch, you owe it to yourself to visit some of the Highlands' smaller golfing pleasures. These include Brora, which has a full-time greenskeeping force of sheep and cattle; Tain, which features an Alps hole (which the locals call the Dolly Parton hole, as the second shot must be played blind over two large mounds); and Golspie, a combination inland and links course whose players have battled erosion along the course's shore holes by building massive stone piles. If Lorne were to play a hundred rounds of golf in the Highlands, however, seventy would be at Dornoch. "Everyone has a spiritual home," Lorne concluded. "Dornoch is mine."

LORNE RUBENSTEIN has written a golf column for *The Globe and Mail*, Canada's national newspaper, since 1980. He's written ten books, including *A Season in Dornoch, Links: An Insider's Tour through the World of Golf*, and books with Nick Price, David Leadbetter, and the late Canadian golfer and master ball-striker, George Knudson. Lorne writes a regular column for *ScoreGolf*, a national publication in Canada, and has written for magazines around the world, including *Golf, Golf World, Golf Digest, Golf Journal, LINKS, Esquire, Travel & Leisure Golf*, and *Cigar Aficionado*. He is a four-time winner of the Golf Writers Association of America annual awards contest.

If You Go

▶ **Getting There:** Dornoch is approximately forty-five minutes north of Inverness, in the Scottish Highlands. Inverness is served via London and Edinburgh by Flybe (+44 139 226-8513; www.flybe.com). Scotrail (+44 845 755-0033; www.nationalrail.co.uk) has service to Dornoch on routes from around Scotland.

▶ **Course Information:** Royal Dornoch (+44 186 281-0219; www.royaldornoch.com) plays 6,704 yards from the blue tees to a par 70. Green fees range from £54 to £92, depending on the season.

▶ **Accommodations:** The Royal Dornoch website (www.royaldornoch.com) includes links to a range of lodging options in town.

DESTINATION

38

THE MACHRIE GOLF LINKS

RECOMMENDED BY **Colin Dalgleish**

If Askernish Old (page 183) is the hidden wonder of the Outer Hebrides, The Machrie Golf Links is the toast of the Inner Hebrides. "The Machrie is a fabulous links, with humps and bumps and beautiful turf, situated in an out-of-this-world location along a magnificent beach on the malt-whisky island of Islay," Colin Dalgleish effused. "My company books hundreds of guests each year who want to visit the British Isles to play golf, but few make it to The Machrie, as they're more interested in ticking off the courses they're familiar with. I am extremely fortunate in that I have played many of the world's greatest courses, but The Machrie is my favorite place to go with friends for 'away-from-it-all' golf. It's twenty minutes in the air from Glasgow, and it's another world."

Islay is the southernmost island in the Inner Hebrides chain, roughly two hours by ferry from the mainland; it's far enough south that on a clear day, you can spy the coast of Northern Ireland. Those unacquainted with the island may have some familiarity with its primary export—single-malt whisky. There are eight distilleries in operation on Islay, including Ardbeg, Lagavulin, and Laphroaig; the oldest operating distillery, Bowmore, was established in 1779. Golf on the island only goes back to 1891, when Willie Campbell, a competitive player and club maker who hailed from Musselburgh, laid out the course that players largely see today; some modifications were made in the 1980s by Donald Steel. The Machrie gained notoriety early in its life, when it hosted an exhibition match between the great triumvirate of British golf of the day—Harry Vardon, John Henry Taylor, and James Braid. Dubbed the Western Isles Open, the match had first-prize money of £100 (worth £6,650 today)—the largest prize of its kind in the British Isles. "The purse was put up by the distillers, partly to attract attention to their product," Colin explained. "Oddly enough, the [British] Open had been held the week before over at

OPPOSITE:
The Machrie, on the whisky isle of Islay, is marked by an abundance of blind shots.

Muirfield, and the first prize there was only £20!" That match was won by J. H. Taylor after Braid's putt to half the final hole was deflected past the hole by a piece of sheep dung—a true links experience!

The Machrie has everything that players love about Scottish links courses—rumpled fairways, wind-blasted dunes, and long seaward vistas. It also has more than its fair share of what some despise—blind shots. In his fine book, *Blasted Heaths and Blessed Greens*, James Finnegan said this of The Machrie:

> Of the 35 full shots thus to be played by a low-handicap golfer, nine are likely to be blind! Yes, it is excessive, this astounding eighteen at Machrie. But I insist that the excess is justified, first on the grounds of sheer golfing fun (to say nothing of the challenge to both our psyche and our swing!) And second on historical grounds. The course is a bona fide relic, not so old as North Berwick or Prestwick, but, like them both, a price-less example of the way golf courses were brought into being.

"Every course plays easier if you have a familiarity with how the holes unfold, but this is especially true at The Machrie," Colin continued. "I believe that you almost need to take a snapshot of the course in your mind as you play the first time, and play accordingly thereafter. There's always a little uncertainty where you need to hit it, and that does put some people off. In all the times I've played The Machrie, I've never been out there with a scorecard. It's really a match-play kind of course. When I take friends up there, we always stay a night or two and play at least two or three rounds. One time around doesn't do The Machrie justice. Everyone always comes away thinking it's fantastic."

There are a number of holes that Colin looks forward to playing on his two or three trips each year to The Machrie. "The 7th, 8th, and 9th run right along the beach," he said, "with the waves crashing along the left. Of these spectacular seaside holes, the par 4 9th stands out. You hit your tee shot on a slight angle to a plateaued fairway. If you hit to the right side, you have a hanging lie and a blind second shot. If you hit to the middle plateau, you'll see the flag for your second shot, 150 yards or so away. If you're on the left, you have the best placement to work the ball into the green, but you're skirting with the beach. Number 12 is a par 3, about 180 yards, with hills in the background. From the green, you can look across acres and acres of peat bogs. Seventeen is called Ifrinn, Gaelic for 'devil.' The hole is only 350 yards long and the tee shot is very straightforward, but the second shot is completely blind, up and over a massive sand dune. Beyond the location and lay-out, I also appreciate the turf at The Machrie. I don't know if I've ever found a better turf for hitting a crisp iron shot."

Islay has its attractions beyond golf. Single-malt aficionados visit the island to tour the distilleries—at least a several-day endeavor, even for less modest imbibers. Birders are also drawn here to view some of the two hundred species that pass through or call Islay home. There are standing stones and other archeological structures, some dating back to 2,000 B.C. But golfers may not feel the need to wander far beyond The Machrie. "The lodge is in an old farmhouse," Colin said. "It's not five-star, but it's comfortable, very friendly, and the restaurant serves good, wholesome food. We usually fall out of bed, play golf, take a shower, have dinner, drink a few single-malts in the little bar (which is stocked with every possible Islay whisky), and talk about our rounds, go to bed, and do the same thing the next day. In a world where life is controlled by starting times, it's pure golf."

COLIN DALGLEISH is a founding director of Perry Golf, a leading provider of golf travel to Scotland, England and Wales, Ireland, France, Spain and Portugal, Italy, South Africa, Australia, New Zealand, and China. A native of Helensburgh, Scotland, Colin attended Ohio State University and graduated from Stirling University in Scotland with a B.A. degree in accounting. He was the Scottish Amateur Champion in 1981, and was a member of the Great Britain and Ireland Walker Cup Team that year. Colin was appointed captain of the GB&I Walker Cup Team for the 2007 Match at Royal County Down and the 2009 Match at Merion.

If You Go

▶ **Getting There:** Machrie is in the town of Port Ellen on the island of Islay. Flights are available from Glasgow on British Airways (800-247-9297; www.ba.com). You can also take a ferry from Kennacraig to Port Ellen on CalMac (+44 800 066 5000; www.calmac.co.uk).

▶ **Course Information:** Machrie Golf Links plays a modest 6,250 yards from the men's tees to a par 71. Visitor green fees range from £20 to £55, depending on the time of year.

▶ **Accommodations:** There's a hotel on site at The Machrie (+44 149 630 2310; www.machrie.com) that offers a variety of rooms, a welcoming pub, and a full dinner menu.

MACHRIHANISH GOLF CLUB

RECOMMENDED BY **Brian Morgan**

Brian Morgan's introduction to Machrihanish Golf Club came in the 1960s, a scant ninety years into the club's existence. "I was a member of the Erskine Golf Club, on the banks of the River Clyde, ten miles west of Glasgow," Brian began. "Every year, the club would have an outing over to Machrihanish. The drive from Glasgow is about three hours—a wonderful scenic drive. You go along the side of Loch Lomond, turn west at Tarbet, go up and over the "rest and be thankfull" (a famous hill) and down and around the start of Loch Fyne to Inverary. About halfway, there's one of the finest seafood restaurants in the world, the Loch Fyne Oyster Bar (in Cairndow), where we stop for lunch. After lunch, we head down the shores of Loch Fyne and eventually cross over to the Atlantic side of the peninsula for the last twenty-five miles to Machrihanish along the spectacular coast, with views of the islands of Ghia and Islay and the Paps of Jura. We'd get there in time to play a round of golf in the late afternoon, then we'd play again in the morning and head home—often stopping for lunch again at the Oyster Bar. The appeal for me is that Machrihanish seems to have changed very little from its incarnation. There are some blind holes, some crooked holes—very true to the old links style. The course rests very naturally in the land. It's not the most difficult track you'll play, but it's certainly great fun. I've been going back every year since my first visit."

The village of Machrihanish (population 500) and its golf course lie near the southern end of the Kintyre peninsula, on the west coast abreast the Atlantic. At the bottom of the forty-mile peninsula rests the Mull (headlands) of Kintyre, which is just twelve miles from the coast of Northern Ireland (and was immortalized by Paul McCartney and his post-Beatles band Wings in 1977 in a song of the same name.) Historians believe that the peninsula once served as a land bridge between Scotland and Ireland, and that the Celtic

OPPOSITE:

Coming upon Machrihanish in 1879, Old Tom Morris said, "The Almichty maun hae had gowf in his e'e when he made this place!"

DESTINATION

40

179

Gaels who settled the region of Argyll (which includes Kintyre) crossed over here. Today, most of the traffic comes from the north, increasingly in the shape of aficionados who have heard tales of the unblemished links here—though its relative remoteness has prevented the course from becoming too crowded.

Locals began playing golf in Machrihanish as early as 1871, when ten holes were laid out. When the club officially formed in 1876 (as the Kintyre Golf Club), two more holes were added. The estimable Old Tom Morris arrived in 1879 and added a final six holes, and re-purposed the routing to what players (for the most part) see today. The story goes that when he saw the site, Morris exclaimed, "The Almichty maun hae had gowf in his e'e when he made this place!" Considering his active playing schedule, his club-making activities, and his stints as greenskeeper at Prestwick and St. Andrews, one can't help but wonder how Morris could have squeezed in so many formidable designs—Carnoustie, Crail, Cruden Bay, Lahinch, Muirfield, Nairn, Prestwick, Rosapenna, Royal County Down, Royal Dornoch, and St. Andrews (New) among them. Golf writer Kevin Cook has pointed out that Morris's design regimen was not quite as rigorous as those adopted by Tom Doak or Bill Coore, who might spend weeks or months walking a site and a year (or more) overseeing construction. For his £1-a-day fee, "Morris would walk the links, saying, 'Put a green there, a bunker here,' and finish by lunchtime."

However fleeting his time may have been while routing Machrihanish, most feel that his fee was more than justified on the first hole alone. "The locals claim it's the top opening hole in golf," Brian offered; many outsiders agree. This cape hole plays 436 yards from the back tee, and requires the player to fly a good deal of beach to reach the fairway on the other side. "The wind comes in from the water," Brian continued, "and if you play it too safe, you will find yourself nearly to the 18th fairway with a very long second shot." Local rules, one should note, allow you to play the beach as a lateral hazard, which should encourage players to be a bit more aggressive. After all, what more authentic links experience could you hope for than hitting your approach from an *actual* beach? For Brian, another standout hole is the 360-yard par 4 8th. "You play from an elevated tee to a flat fairway and up to an elevated green," he described. "If your approach is long, you roll far off; if you're short, you roll back down. The view from the tee is one of the great views of golf—there's the fairway, then the sea, then the Paps of Jura [three mountains that reach over 2,000 feet on the island of Jura]. It's as if you're looking into the mouth of a T. rex."

Like any links course worth its mettle, Machrihanish is not immune to the vicissitudes of the wind. Brian recalled an occasion when the gales blowing in off the Atlantic were particularly virulent. "I had taken a friend who's a member at Augusta National over to Machrihanish, and we were on the 10th tee, a long par 5. My friend teed it up a little higher than he should've, and he popped his tee shot up. The ball went about five yards out and twenty feet up in the air—and the wind blew the ball twenty feet behind him. I've been in the clubhouse with him at Augusta since, and he still enjoys telling other members how with the help of the wind, he managed to hit a golf ball backward in Scotland."

Brian Morgan's love of Machrihanish runs deep, and he expressed his affection for the place by helping to create a new course there. "About twenty years ago, I spied a piece of undeveloped links land right next to Machrihanish and thought it had all the properties that would make an excellent companion course," Brian said. "I wasn't in a position then to do anything about it, but it was always in the back of my mind. Five years ago, I was finally able to bring together some partners to fund the project and negotiate an arrangement with the farmer who I had managed to get to agree to an option years before. Now the course has happened. David McLay Kidd (of Bandon Dunes fame) did the layout, and Machrihanish Dunes opened for play in the spring of 2009."

BRIAN MORGAN is one of the world's leading golf photographers. His portfolio—culled from over fifty years of shooting—includes over a million golf images from around the world—candid shots of golf personalities, major events, and course landscapes. Some examples of his work can be viewed at www.brianmorgan.com.

If You Go

▶ **Getting There:** Machrihanish Golf Club is approximately three hours' drive from Glasgow, which is served by most major carriers. Daily flights are available from Glasgow to nearby Campbeltown via Loganair (+44 845 773-3377; www.loganair.co.uk).

▶ **Course Information:** Machrihanish (+44 158 681-0213; www.machgolf.com) plays 6,462 yards from the blues to a par 70. Green fees range from £25 to £60.

▶ **Accommodations:** The Machrihanish Golf Club website (www.machgolf.com) lists a range of lodging options in the town of Machrihanish.

DESTINATION

40

ASKERNISH OLD

RECOMMENDED BY **John Garrity**

Back in 1990, John Garrity experienced the thrill of discovery in a very profound way, uncovering an 1891 Old Tom Morris design on the isolated Scottish island of South Uist. The course, Askernish, had not simply eluded American visitors. It had literally been lost to the ages!

"I was on my first overseas golf assignment for *Sports Illustrated*," John recalled, "to do a piece on the Royal and Ancient. To make trips abroad cost-effective, the magazine would assign writers several pieces germane to the region we were visiting. In addition to the St. Andrews essay, they asked me to explore an Old Tom Morris course that was supposed to exist out in the Hebrides. The thinking was it would be very close to a time machine, and would illustrate what a genuine Scottish links course would have been like in the 1890s. It was a long voyage out to the island of South Uist, and when I finally reached the course in question, it was very evident that Tom Morris had not been remotely involved. It was a meadow with dead crows hanging from a surrounding fence. I saw something that looked like a tee, teed up a ball and hit out toward Newfoundland. I eventually found the ball and walked forward to see if there was anything that looked like a green. I found a green site, threw my hat down to mark the spot and returned to try to find my ball. It couldn't be found, so I dropped another and hit.

"As we were playing, a truck arrived carrying two guys with a lawnmower and a flag. They started mowing grass behind us. A little while later, the 9th hole appeared. We soon learned that this little nine-holer disappeared each winter. The greenskeeper was a chef at a local hotel. Old Tom Morris or not, we spent several days there and had a pleasant time. The course had a little hand-drawn scorecard with a map of the course. It showed two tees for each of the nine, but I could never find the alternate 9th tee. I was determined to find

OPPOSITE:
The long-forgotten Old Tom Morris layout at "Askernish Old" unfolded from behind the dunes of the 9th tee on "Askernish New," drawing John Garrity—and soon thousands of others—to the remote island of South Uist.

DESTINATION

41

it, and wondered if it could be up on a dune in a corner of the meadow. We walked up, and that's where it was. It held no interest for me, however, when I saw what was south— a stretch of land that looked like Ballybunion, only more severe. This was the only point on the nine-hole course where you could see this land—the land, I was certain, where Tom Morris had built his course.

"As it was only May, the grass hadn't grown very high, and I decided to play it. From the tee, I could see what appeared to be a fairway, the sea to the right, mountains to the left. I hit a two-iron, and then pitched up to a natural green site. I gave myself two putts, then scrambled up to the top of the next dune, where I could make out another hole. It was just me, *Sports Illustrated* photographer Lane Stewart, a dead sheep, and lots of rabbits—or at least lots of rabbit holes. I continued for six or eight holes, playing golf very much the way the ancient players did—in the early days, you found your own 'course,' following the contours of the land as you saw fit. I called this course 'Askernish Old' in my story, and I called the nine-holer 'Askernish New.' The story always had a special place in my heart, one of my first big assignments as a golf writer. I never heard anything back from Scotland; Askernish Old seemed to have gone lost again in my absence. I, however, never forgot about the course. It was always in my mind that I'd get back there, though it never happened."

John indeed had rediscovered a lost Old Tom Morris design. A magazine account by Morris's friend and frequent companion, Horace Hutchinson, made mention of Morris's trip to South Uist, and the layout of eighteen holes on "the rolling dunes of Askernish Farm." For a few decades, the course was played regularly by visitors and more affluent locals; it was maintained by farmers using scythes. When the land fell back into agricultural use in the twenties (under the complexities of Scottish crofting law), the course began reverting to its pre-golf state. It was consigned to further oblivion when a local hotelier commissioned a twelve-hole course to be built on the flatter land adjacent, in large part because it could be easily maintained with grass-cutting equipment that was used to keep the local airstrip (also nearby) in shape.

John's story picks up some seventeen years later. "I was sitting in the press room at the U.S. Open in Oakmont [in 2007], checking email," John continued. "There was one from the office saying that someone was trying to reach me from Askernish, Scotland—a Ralph Thompson. I had a good idea of why he had called. I'd recently done a little satirical column on the Golf.com Website, listing my top fifty courses. It was set up to look very scientific, though if you looked closely, courses were ranked upon my having had memorable experiences on them. Poipu Bay was on the list, as I had played a pro-am with Tiger Woods and we'd won! Number one on the list was Askernish Old—my conceit being that the course didn't really exist—at least not anymore. Or so I thought.

"I called Ralph Thompson from the press room and he picked up in two rings. I was ready to confess my little joke, when he explained how the folks at Askernish were beside themselves that people were already discovering them, and the course wasn't even quite ready to open. Ready to open? I was shocked as he explained how someone else (a golf consultant named Gordon Irvine) had stumbled upon Askernish Old, and with the help of designer Martin Ebert, the course was being rebuilt. Ralph invited me to visit and be among the first golfers to play it in its new incarnation.

"When I visited in the spring of 2008, the course wasn't quite playable—fifteen holes were open, but if you missed the fairway, you were lost. There were more rabbit burrows—deeper than I remembered—but the Old Tom Morris greens had reappeared. The new holes that Ebert had built were pretty good—but the course really begins on the 7th, where you look out on this otherworldly dunes landscape with fairways snaking through. We got to play two days—me and a group of potential investors—and on the second day I made history . . . or so I thought. We were playing the par 4 15th hole, called Old Tom's Pulpit. It has a bizarre green—the front juts out like a pulpit, with a punchbowl behind the pulpit. I hit a gap wedge or nine-iron in, and when I got up there, people on the green said, 'You're in the hole!' I was very excited—I thought I'd notched the first eagle on the reinvigorated Askernish Old. Then they broke my heart: my ball was in a rabbit hole, not the flagstick hole."

It's unknown at this time if the first eagle has been notched at Old Tom's Pulpit. But if by any strange circumstance Askernish Old should go missing again, John Garrity has generously volunteered to help club members locate the lost links.

John Garrity is a senior writer for *Sports Illustrated*, where he's worked since 1979. At *SI*, he has covered many sports, but his beat has been golf since 1989. A Golf Writers Association of America multiple-award-winner, John is also a regular contributor to *Golf* magazine and *Travel & Leisure Golf*, among other publications. He's authored over a dozen books, including *Tiger 2.0* and his most recent title, *Ancestral Links*.

If You Go

▶ **Getting There:** Askernish Golf Club is on the island of South Uist in the Outer Hebrides islands off the northwest coast of Scotland. Flights are available from Glasgow to Benbecula (on North Uist island) on British Airways (800-247-9297; www.ba.com). You can also take a ferry from the mainland to The Uists on CalMac (+44 8000 66 5000; www.calmac.co.uk.

▶ **Course Information:** Askernish Golf Club (+44 7900 387167; www.askernishgolf-club.com) plays 6,128 yards from the men's tees, to a par 72. Green fees are £25.

▶ **Accommodations:** The Askernish Website (www.askernishgolfclub.com) lists the range of lodging options available on South Uist.

DURBAN COUNTRY CLUB

RECOMMENDED BY **Gordon Turner**

The anxieties that have struck countless golfers approaching the first tee at Durban Country Club struck home for Gordon Turner at the tender age of nine, before he'd even lifted a club.

"Growing up in a farming community outside of the city, it was always the greatest treat to be invited for Sunday lunch at Durban Country Club," Gordon began. "As guests of my great-aunt, a lifelong member of this most colonial of establishments, my brother and I would be scrubbed clean and clothed in our Sunday finest (with shoes) for the trek in from the sugar plantations. Although the imposing Cape Dutch clubhouse and the beady eye of the huge Zulu doorman were enough to keep us in check, the journey would always end with a stern reminder from Dad that farm etiquette would not be accepted on Country Club property. My clearest memory of those visits is of sitting with my nose pressed against the bay window above the 1st tee, ignoring the adult-speak at the table, trying to fathom the nervousness being exhibited by group after group of grown men as they lined up their drives. It wasn't long into my golfing life that I had to deal with my own demons on that opening hole."

With the shackles of apartheid largely cast off, South Africa is being recognized as a must-go travel destination, thanks to breathtakingly diverse scenery, incredible wildlife-viewing opportunities, a burgeoning wine industry, and excellent golf in a variety of environs. There's Royal Cape Golf Club in the shadow of Table Mountain in Cape Town; the links course at Fancourt and Pinnacle Point, both to the east of Cape Town on the famed Garden Route; and Leopard Creek, a Gary Player design that borders Kruger National Park. But of all the courses South Africa offers, Durban Country Club, in the KwaZulu-Natal province on the country's northeastern coast, is considered the grande

dame. It came into being in 1922 largely due to the misfortunes of Royal Durban, a course prone to flooding. Royal Durban was the site of the 1919 South African Open, a waterlogged mess, and town fathers feared that their city would be overlooked on the national tournament circuit if changes weren't made. Their response was to commission George Waterman and Laurie Waters (a champion player of the day) to design the Country Club of Durban on a spit of dunesy land overlooking the Blue Lagoon estuary and Indian Ocean. The course was dry enough—and challenging enough—to host the 1924 Open and fifteen more since, more than any other club. It was here that Gary Player won his first South African Open in 1956, and nearly all the country's golf luminaries have passed through since. Player returned in 1990, this time to refurbish the grande dame as she approached seventy.

A few years after watching the grown-ups teeing off, Gordon had his first game at Durban—the first of hundreds of rounds. The course still makes a grand impression. "It's rolling land, moving north to south," he described. "It's a hard course to characterize, as it's not exactly links, not exactly parkland. It's somewhat akin to the kind of terrain you find in the Melbourne Sandbelt. The greens and fairways use a hybrid grass that was created just for the club. The green sites are generally small, flat, well bunkered, and perched in precarious positions. If you're having a bad round, you can find yourself reloading all day. As far as I'm concerned, it's tough to beat the first five holes at Durban— they're about as good as it gets. The tee boxes are perched high, and you hit down chutes into valleys of dunes. It could be Royal County Down [in Northern Ireland], except instead of fescue grasses, you have banana and palm trees. And you don't want to wander too far into the bush after your ball, as there are a number of poisonous snakes in this region— black mamba, green mamba, and Mozambique spitting cobra.

"On the 1st, the tee box aims you a little right, the hole bends a little left, and the green sits perched amongst the thick coastal bush that frames most holes, at the end of a narrow band of rolling fairway. It's not a particularly long hole, just a 3-wood and a 9-iron for most, yet it's as intimidating an opening hole as you will find, as the right side is all out of bounds and the left is bush. With a constant sea breeze coming at or behind your right shoulder, everything screams: 'Don't go right!' and before you know it you are in cobra country up the left side, scrambling for par. This opener immediately puts the golfer on edge and prepares you for the challenge ahead. The sea view from the elevated tee on the par 3 2nd hole is outstanding, but the shot is demanding; anything that's not on the green

OPPOSITE:
Many matches turn on the short par 4 18th at Durban Country Club.

DESTINATION

42

will either be in a bunker or roll down the green's front slope. And then there's the fear and loathing of the 3rd hole."

Some have called the perspective from the tee at the 512-yard par 5 3rd at Durban the most frightening view in golf. (Architect Tom Doak has equated the vision with "looking down the barrel of a gun.") The tee is suspended sixty feet above a narrow, undulating fairway, with dense bush on the right (don't forget the snakes!), dunes on the left, and a long, narrow bunker that juts ever so slightly into the fairway on the left side. "When you're up on the tee, you don't know where to hit it," Gordon continued. "There's just a little sliver of green to aim for. It's not really that difficult a hole, so long as you keep your drive in bounds. If you don't, it's not hard to take a 9. The opening sequence ends with par 3 into a bowl-like green, and the demanding par 4 5th."

While the first five holes show Durban at its very best, the remaining thirteen holes are remarkably good. A few that stand out for Gordon include the 12th, the 17th, and the 18th. "From the 11th green, you walk to the top of a dune, and you're hitting to another little dune, a little pimple of a green. It's not long—158 yards. But if you don't hit a good shot, you can play volleyball back and forth, bunker to bunker, all day long. It's been called the Prince of Wales hole, as Prince Edward is said to have taken a 16 on the hole in 1924. The par 4 17th is a bit like playing golf on the moon. It sits low in the bush, and the fairway travels up and down a large dune, then plays up to a little green site on top of another dune. Eighteen is one of those holes that everyone has a comment on. It's only 275 yards—there's a drop-off on the right side, bush on the left, and the clubhouse right behind. Everything encourages you to go for it—why come all this way and not try it? You see a lot of birdies and a lot of doubles. Many matches turn here."

GORDON TURNER grew up in Durban, cutting his golfing teeth at Royal Durban and Durban Country Club. Fortunate to play with and against Tim Clark and Rory Sabbatini as a junior, Gordon quickly realized that he would go hungry if forced to earn a living against such talents. He now oversees South African operations for Perry Golf. Gordon is part of the Golf Digest panel for the Top 100 courses and has been fortunate to play on many of the world's finest layouts. He is married to Nicky, has a son, Cameron, and a daughter, Ella, and resides in Cape Town.

If You Go

▶ **Getting There:** Durban Country Club is close to the center of Durban, which is served from Johannesburg or Cape Town by South African Airways (+27 11 978-5313; www.flyssa. com). Johannesburg and Cape Town are served by many major carriers, including Swiss Air (877-359-7947; www.swiss.com), BMI (+44 133 285-4854; www.flybmi.com), and South African Airways.

▶ **Course Information:** Royal Durban Country Club (+27 31 313-1777; www.dcclub.co.za) plays 6,720 yards from the back tees to a par 72. The course is open to visitor play most weekdays; green fees are between 350 and 500 rand (at press time, approximately $35 to $50).

▶ **Accommodations:** Tourism KwaZulu-Natal (+27 31 366-7500; www.durban.kzn.org. za) lists accommodations in greater Durban. "Tourists don't often think of a stay in Durban," Gordon said, "but there's rich colonial history, great multiculturalism, fantastic beaches, great diving an hour south, and the game reserves just three hours north."

KIAWAH ISLAND (THE OCEAN COURSE)

RECOMMENDED BY **Hunki Yun**

The notion of "resort course" implies an easier golf course, the kind of track where thrice-a-year players can limit their ball loss to less than a dozen, and where clients on a vendor-sponsored retreat can come away feeling good about their game (and, with luck, about signing on the dotted line for next year's order).

The Ocean Course—one of five at Kiawah Island, just south of Charleston, South Carolina—is not that sort of resort course.

"I used to work for *Golf Digest,* and covered the 'college golf' beat," Hunki Yun said. "I was sent down to Hilton Head to cover the Palmetto Dunes Collegiate Invitational, and snuck away one day to play the Ocean Course. It was unlike anything I had every played before in the United States. It was the first manufactured links course that looked like it had been there for decades. Courses like Chambers Bay and Whistling Straits owe their ancestry to the Ocean Course."

When Pete and Alice Dye received the nod at Kiawah to create a venue for the 1991 Ryder Cup match, they were given one of the finest pieces of golf land available on the eastern United States. The Ocean Course lies on the southeastern tip of the 10,000-acre barrier island, providing both ample dunes and access to ocean views. As an added bonus, the course would be spared residences, providing for a pure golf experience. Much of the "manufacture" of the Ocean Course comes from the decision (credited to Alice) to build up the fairways of the holes that would rest away from the Atlantic so that every hole would afford an ocean view—some by as much as eight feet. Though this feat required a massive movement of earth, most visitors would hardly notice. Indeed, guests frequently comment on the "naturalness" of the course. The result is ten holes adjoining the Atlantic (more seaside holes than any course in the Northern Hemisphere, Kiawah

OPPOSITE:
Uncompromising
tidal marsh
carries help
differentiate the
Ocean Course
from traditional
links layouts.

DESTINATION

43

193

Resort's promotional literature points out) and eight more running parallel, one fairway removed from the sea.

When the European team arrived at Kiawah in 1991, what they found was not exactly a replica of their home links courses (albeit with more sunshine), though the Ocean Course certainly can at times have a links feel. There are large waste bunkers that seem to spill out of the dunes (in some cases they do), billowing fescue adorning the bunkers, and carry areas off the tees. (The sand, incidentally, is played as a natural hazard, so your club can be grounded.) On the holes adjoining the beach, the sparse trees have been bent by the wind, and the whiff of sea spray is everpresent. The Ocean departs from a links orientation with its incessant and uncompromising tidal marsh carries and the abrupt fall-off from the elevated fairways should you miss. The fairways are also lusher than you'd find at a genuine links, and don't always give players a friendly roll. "Not everyone who comes to the Ocean Course is the kind of serious golfer who might make the trip to Ireland for that style of rough-and-ready golf," Hunky continued. "If you're not a student of links golf and you're paying $300-plus for a round, you expect pristine conditioning. Relative to most links I've played overseas, I'd say that everything at Kiawah is on a bigger scale—the waste bunkers are bigger, there are more cross hazards, the carries off the tee longer, the wind fiercer. All this combines to make it a very difficult course." Since the course's inauguration, Pete Dye has returned to Kiawah twice to tone down the Ocean's rougher edges, adding a new set of tees geared for the mid-handicapper at around 6,400 yards, and planting turf in the recovery areas around the green sites where sandy waste once awaited missed approaches.

Hunki made mention of the wind, and this facet of the playing experience at Kiawah can't be overemphasized. Dye's figure-eight layout essentially eliminates any notion of a prevailing wind. It can come from the east or the west, or both. One thing you can count on is that it will be strong; course notes claim as much as an eight-club difference from one day to the next. Perhaps this is an exaggeration, but Hunki pointed out that he'd "hate to have to post a score after going out on a late afternoon in the spring when the wind's at its worst!"

As Ryder Cup competitors learned in 1991—and as visitors new and old discover every day—there are few tougher finishes in golf than the last five holes on the Ocean. Of these, the final two holes have garnered the greatest notoriety. "During the Ryder Cup match, 17 [a 197-yard par 3] seemed to befuddle the players," Hunki opined. "It's all water carry, there's water to the right of the green, big bunkers on the left, and sea oaks and dunes behind. You're often hitting right into the wind. I think the 17th is the Ocean's most famous hole because of the way the pros butchered it in 1991—anyone who saw the tourney or the highlight clips cannot forget Mark Calvechia's shank into the lake. To navigate this hole, you have to think clearly, pick the right club, and execute. Without doing all three, there's no way you'll be on the green putting for birdie." Or as Pete Dye put it, "Any dry shot is a good shot on this hole."

Calvechia, Ballesteros and other '91 competitors will find the 18th somewhat different—and to most minds improved. In 2002 the green was moved from a set of artificial dunes to a point twenty-five yards closer to the Atlantic, along the land's natural dune line. The change added just a few yards to this intimidating 439-yard par 4 but, more significantly, greatly enhanced the second shot, which now provides a panoramic backdrop of the ocean and dunes. "You usually hit your approach with the wind coming in off the ocean," Hunki added. "I can't think of any better finish." Putting out on the 18th is topped off by a visit to the new clubhouse. "It has a Maidstone feeling, and looks as though it belongs in the Hamptons. There are wraparound windows in the grill. It's one of my favorite spots to have a drink after a round. They got all the touches right."

Hunki Yun is editor of *LINKS* magazine.

If You Go

▶ **Getting There:** Kiawah Island is thirty-three miles from the Charleston, South Carolina, International Airport, which is served by most major carriers.

▶ **Course Information:** The Ocean Course (800-654-2924; www.kiawahresort.com) plays 7,356 yards from the tournament tees to a par 72; it has a slope rating of 144. Green fees are $350.

▶ **Accommodations:** Visitors to Kiawah (800-654-2924; www.kiawahresort.com) can choose from the recently opened Sanctuary Hotel or a collection of rental villas.

DESTINATION

43

PGA GOLF DE CATALUNYA (GREEN)

RECOMMENDED BY **Gene A. Holland, Jr.**

Sometimes golfers find interesting new courses in slightly roundabout ways. Gene Holland's quest for fine wine—or at least some golf courses in proximity to fine wine—eventually led him to PGA Golf de Catalunya.

"When Jim Dondero and I decided to start an upscale epicurean golf travel company, we attended the PGA Merchandising Show in Orlando (the show is held each January)," Gene began. "We wanted to get a sense of what venues might be a good match for what we hoped to offer our clients. The Spanish Tourism Board was exhibiting at the event, and we stopped by to chat. I have to admit that I didn't know too much about Spanish golf beyond Valderrama and Sotogrande. We were asking about quality golf venues in the La Rioja region, as the fine vintages coming from there would cover the wine-tasting side of a visit. The representative said that there was no golf to speak of in Rioja, but good golf a bit east in the region of Catalonia—at PGA Golf de Catalunya. I'd never heard of it and had been around a bit, but I made a mental note. When we went to Spain and France later that year, we played the Green Course (the resort's tournament venue), as we visit all of the destinations that we represent. While it doesn't have all the grand trappings of a private club like Valderrama, it was as close to pure golf as you can find on the Continent. The standards of course maintenance are a little bit different in Spain than in the States. When you get away from the very top rung of courses, you get a rapid drop in quality. When we see a course built and maintained to U.S. standards, it catches our attention."

Spain is not an unknown destination for golf travelers. British and Irish citizens frequently find their way to Costa del Sol in the south for an infusion of vitamin D and mild-weather golf. Catalonia and its largest city, Barcelona, see far fewer golf visitors, though many flock here to frolic on the beaches of the Costa Brava, which stretch north from

Barcelona. Catalonia lacks the depth of courses that Costa del Sol can claim, and for some this speaks in the region's favor. "There are some wonderful courses in the south with great vistas of the Mediterranean," Gene continued, "but there are times when your tee shots are framed by rows of condos. Barcelona is a genuine Mediterranean city and affords visitors a more authentic experience. After a few days in Barcelona, a visit to Catalunya is a fine escape to the bucolic countryside of the Costa Brava."

PGA Golf de Catalunya is the creation of PGA European Tour Courses, an entity that was initially formed as a joint venture between the sports marketing group IMG and the PGA European Tour. The company owns and manages a network of courses across Europe with the goal of building and maintaining properties of a quality that could host a major tourney. The company's holdings include courses in Portugal, Germany, Norway, Finland, Estonia, and Ireland. The two courses at Catalunya were laid out by European Tour professionals Neil Coles and Angel Gallardo, who between them hold twenty-five European Tour titles. (Coles also shares a distinction with Sam Snead, being the only other player to win a professional tournament in six different decades.) "The Green Course at Catalunya is a parkland layout, with dense stands of cork oaks and umbrella pines," Gene said. "There are several lakes on the property, and vistas of distant mountains. Overall, it's a challenging design, but not overly finicky.

"I found the series of holes from 11 through 13, which approach and work their way around one of the lakes, especially compelling. The 11th is a 190-yard par 3, and plays downhill with a drop of forty feet to a large green. It's more visually intimidating than actually difficult, so long as you make note to club accordingly, as the lake begins behind the green. Number 12 is a 540-yard par 5, working gently uphill. You play your tee shot over the corner of the lake. There's a large cork tree that guards the green on the left; if you're too close to the tree, your approach is blocked, so you have to think the second shot through carefully. The 402-yard par 4 13th comes back downhill toward the lake; there's a superb view from the tee of the course and surrounding countryside. The green sits up on a little plateau and has water in front, water to the right, and water behind. There's a great premium to hitting the fairway on this hole, even if it means hitting a fairway wood or long-iron off the tee, as you don't want to try to hit this green from the rough."

Catalunya is not the sole club of interest in greater Barcelona. Thirty minutes west of the city is Real Club de Golf El Prat. This club used to be near the beach, but was moved recently to its current location in rolling countryside near the town of Terrassa, where

Greg Norman Design constructed forty-five holes. "On some courses where you slice and dice nines, the different sets of holes have radically different feelings," Gene observed. "At El Prat you can fashion together many different combinations, but there's a consistent feeling throughout." Gene even found a track worth visiting near Rioja. "There's a little public course up in the forested hills called Izki Golf," Gene added. "It's a Seve Ballesteros design. You may not see top-flight course conditioning here, but it still offers excellent-quality golf in close proximity to one of the world's greatest wine regions."

Before they visit PGA Golf de Catalunya or any other area courses, Gene urges clients to linger a while in Barcelona. "It's simply an amazing city," he effused. "Anyone remotely interested in food needs to experience the tapas bars and La Boqueria, one of the world's great markets. An architectural tour of the city is also in order. Whether you like Antoni Gaudí's work or not, you must see it. One of his buildings—the Sagrada Familia church—has been under construction since 1882, and it's not slated for completion until 2026. However, you can still walk through."

GENE A. HOLLAND, JR. is principal and cofounder of Cork and Tee (www.corkandtee. com), which offers customized epicurean golf travel. He was a member of the varsity golf team at the University of North Carolina at Chapel Hill, where he played with notables such as Davis Love, III and Jack Nicklaus, II. Following his collegiate playing days, Gene spent eleven years as a club professional, earning his PGA Class A membership and honing his skills as a player, golf instructor, and administrator. After receiving his M.B.A. from UNC's Kenan-Flagler Business School, he worked nearly five years as a commercial banker before launching Cork and Tee.

If You Go

▶ **Getting There:** PGA Golf de Catalunya is near the town of Girona, which is sixty-five miles from the airport in Barcelona. Barcelona is served by most major carriers.

▶ **Course Information:** PGA Catalunya plays 7,205 yards from the back tees, to a par 72; it has a slope rating of 138. Green fees range from €67 to €92.

▶ **Accommodations:** The Meliá Golf Vichy Catalán Hotel (+34 972 181 020; www.meliagolfvichycatalan.com) is located in the midst of the Catalunya course.

BLUE CANYON (CANYON COURSE)

RECOMMENDED BY **Mike Lardner**

The island of Phuket lies off the southwestern edge of the Thai peninsula, in the Andaman Sea. Long a vacation retreat for affluent Bangkok residents and other Asian travelers seeking beachside bliss, Phuket has been discovered by European and North American travelers in the last few decades, and is now a regular stop for Westerners making the trek to Thailand. Many come to cruise the waters of Ao Phang-Nga National Park, with its otherworldly islands of karst limestone, or to scuba dive the waters off Ko Phi Phi or the Similan Islands. Increasingly, itinerant golfers are finding their way to Phuket. While it lacks the density of golf courses found around Bangkok, its six venues—The Banyan Tree Golf Club, Mission Hills Golf Club, Loch Palm Golf Club, Phuket Country Club, and the two tracks at Blue Canyon Country Club—offer a high-quality experience and, like the rest of Thailand, a great value. Topmost on people's must-play lists in the region is the Canyon Course at Blue Canyon.

"Back in the early nineties, I was on a cruise ship in the Andaman Sea, and we made a stop in Phuket," Mike Lardner began. "We were hoping to find a good place to play golf for future passengers, and we came across Blue Canyon, conveniently located near our docking spot. Blue Canyon had two spectacular tropical courses—the Canyon and the Lake—carved out of the jungle. There were no ocean vistas, though the site was close enough to the Andaman Sea to get nice breezes (which are welcome in Thailand, as it gets quite hot and humid for most Westerners' tastes). The clubhouse at Blue Canyon is one of the most striking I've ever visited, a Thai-style design with open walls and an open floor plan. Phuket is a unique destination in itself, and a simply magical place to play golf."

Blue Canyon Country Club rests on the former site of a rubber plantation and tin mine—two of Phuket's largest industries before the explosion of tourism. The design for

DESTINATION

45

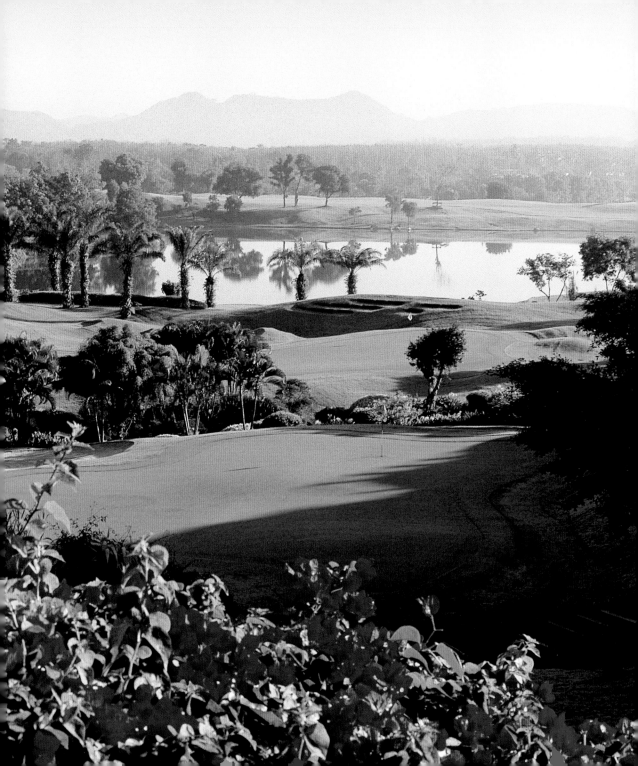

the Canyon Course (and later the Lakes Course) came from Yoshikazo Kato, who moved little dirt (said to be only 250,000 cubic meters) to create the routing. Whereas water comes into play on sixteen holes on the Lakes, players on the Canyon contend with forced carries over the track's namesake canyons and struggle to avoid the woods; water only comes into play on ten holes here. If you can keep it on or near the fairway, you'll be well pampered. "When I've played, the course has been in impeccable condition," Mike continued. "I don't think any expense is spared to keep the course pristine. In my travels around Thailand, I've run into many expatriates. They say that when they get an invite to play Blue Canyon, they do anything they can to make it. That's the reputation the course has."

The Canyon Course is strong from the get-go, but it's on the back that it really shines. Three holes compete for visitors' memory space, beginning with the par 4 13th. Here, players get a real taste of the canyons, as you're required to clear a rather large one. The hole doglegs right, and the canyon extends and widens in the same direction; you can go for it and leave yourself a short-iron home, or play more conservatively for a mid-iron (or longer) shot in. During the 1998 Johnnie Walker Open, Tiger Woods drove the green here while in a playoff against Ernie Els; he had come back from ten strokes behind to tie Els on the final day, and prevailed in the tourney. Standing on the tee considering your own approaching drive, such an accomplishment is mind-boggling; it's known as the Tiger Hole now. The fun continues on the par 3 14th. From an elevated tee, you hit 194 yards (from the back) to a kidney-shaped island green; the ribbon of turf connecting the 14th to the rest of the course has the effect of making the landing area seem even smaller than it is. A second par 3 rounds out Blue Canyon's trilogy of signature holes, the 221-yard 17th. Trees line the left, a lake guards the right, and the green slopes from front to back. At least the hole is slightly downhill to help your shot along.

One constant of golf in Thailand is caddies—female caddies. For Thai women, caddying represents a degree of freedom—they can choose when to work and how much to work. And they can work fewer hours for as much money or more than they might make in other lines of employment, and walk away with their earnings (and hopefully a generous tip) at the end of the round. At Blue Canyon, it's estimated that some 450 area women caddie on the resorts' two courses—swathed head to toe in uniforms and donning a broad-brimmed bonnet to avoid the sun. (In Thai society, a suntan is not considered desirable.) It's not uncommon for players to retain two caddies for a round—one to carry bags, another to carry an umbrella to shield guests from the unrelenting sun. For less

OPPOSITE:
The impeccably
manicured
Canyon Course
is one more
reason to make
the trip to
magical Phuket.

DESTINATION

45

seasoned players, the presence of a caddy can evoke a heightened self-consciousness akin to dread; what 30-handicapper compelled to caddie up at a plush resort course hasn't expected to look back at his looper after a sliced tee shot to find him snickering? In Thailand, there's no need for anxiety, as the general graciousness of Thai people extends to the golf course. Whether you execute or not, you're likely to frequently hear the words "Khaeng raeng"—that is, "Nice shot!"

"I was at Blue Canyon with a group of a dozen visitors in 2007," Mike recalled. "On the first hole, our caddies—young ladies between twenty and thirty—came and lined up for pictures with our guys. The caddies knelt in front, the golfers stood in back; it was very formal. The guests in our group—Americans—were very jovial, and it soon rubbed off on the caddies. By the end of the round, they were high-fiving players in our group. In the photo we took at the end, caddies and players are mixed together, all smiles."

MIKE LARDNER is chairman of Wide World of Golf (www.wideworldofgolf.com), which organizes luxury golf travel around the world.

If You Go

▶ **Getting There:** U.S. visitors can reach Phuket via Bangkok on a number of international carriers, including Japan, Malaysia, Northwest, and United Airlines.

▶ **Course Information:** The Canyon Course at Blue Canyon (+66 76 328 088; www.bluecanyon.com) plays 7,119 yards from the back tees to a par 72; the slope rating is 141. Only visitors staying at Blue Canyon Golfer's Spa Lodge may play the Canyon Course, or those booking tee times through tour operators. Green fees for lodge guests are 3300 baht (approximately $95 USD at press time).

▶ **Accommodations:** The Blue Canyon Golfer's Spa Lodge has thirty-two rooms overlooking the Canyon Course.

ARABIAN RANCHES

RECOMMENDED BY **Ian Baker-Finch**

Dubai is one of seven emirates of the United Arab Emirates, a small and tremendously wealthy nation sandwiched between Saudi Arabia and Oman. Dubai City (often simply referred to as Dubai) is situated on the Persian Gulf, near the eastern edge of the country. Cultural commentators sometimes refer to it as the city of the future, a phrase spoken with a mix of wonder and, one senses, fear. Though it's geographically near the heart of Arabia, Dubai is a wild polyglot of expats and guest workers—only 10 to 15 percent of the population of nearly two million is Arabic. The city has experienced one of the most dramatic growth explosions witnessed anywhere in modern times, as city fathers hope to make it the business and recreation center of the Middle East; much of the city's soaring skyline did not exist ten years ago. It seems anything is possible—given adequate resources and unlimited imagination. This sense of infinite possibility extends to golf.

Golf was introduced to the Arabian Gulf in the early days of the petroleum industry by Americans working in Saudi Arabia for companies like Aramco and Tapline. Water (and hence grass) being in short supply, makeshift courses were created in the midst of the desert, as the late, great golf writer Dick Severino described:

> The balls are red, the greens are brown and the fairways are more like runways. Only the rough lives up to its name. The balls are red because in the glare of the desert sun you can't always see a white ball against the sand and rocks. The greens are brown, or sometimes black, because they are made of oil-treated sand. The fairways are hard because they are made of sand or marl sprayed with oil and compacted to preserve them from the desert wind. As for the rough, one golfer put it this way: "There just ain't nothing else out there."

DESTINATION

46

Regulation-length sand-oil courses were constructed in Saudi Arabia, Bahrain, and Kuwait. The first grass course in the Middle East—meaning grass fairways and greens—did not come into being until 1987. This track, the Majlis course at Emirates Golf Club in Dubai, regularly hosts a PGA European Tour event, the Dubai Desert Classic.

"On my first visit to Dubai, I was surprised to find so many golf courses in the midst of the desert," Ian Baker-Finch recalled. "I was even more surprised to find wall-to-wall grass. The courses were of a parkland style, with lush green grass and trees everywhere. When I spoke to Emmar Properties Chairman Mohamed Ali Alabbar about my vision for a golf course at the Arabian Ranches development, I told him that I wanted to see more desert incorporated in the design. Soon after, we visited one of his botanical gardens to meet with an arborist to discuss what sort of local flora might be available to augment a desert design—one that I imagined would bear more resemblance to a course you might find in Scottsdale or Palm Springs than the early designs I found in Dubai."

With his design at Arabian Ranches, Ian Baker-Finch did not create distinct bunkers; instead, he attempted to incorporate the site's sandy terrain as natural waste areas, this in part to enhance the impression of "fairway as oasis." "Before it became a development and golf course, Arabian Ranches was a camel-and-goat farm," Ian said. "There are native *ghaf* trees on the property [the *ghaf* is a member of the evergreen family, and one of the most robust plants in the desert]. When the camels were present, there was only two or three feet of foliage, all at the top. Once the camels were removed, the foliage grew down nearly to the ground. They add a great perspective to the course, and certainly let you know that you're not in Scottsdale." Thanks to the big winds that blow here, the greens at Arabian Ranches are exceptionally large, to give players a bigger target.

Building a course in the desert poses unique challenges—one that you might anticipate, and one that you might not. "Once you begin moving dirt around and exposing sand, the sand dunes will blow around," Ian described. "I remember being on the site and shaping several holes, only to come back the next day and find that they'd disappeared—they were covered with sand, returning to the desert. It took weeks to recover. We learned that the only way to proceed was to shape one or two holes at a time and intensively grass them. If we did otherwise, they'd go away."

The other problem Ian and the team faced at Arabian Ranches was water—*too much water*—in the wrong places. "I had envisioned the fairways as being lined with native desert areas where an errant shot could be found and chipped back on the short grass,"

OPPOSITE:
Arabian Ranches
is an oasis of
green in the desert
outside Dubai.

DESTINATION

46

Ian explained. "Unfortunately, once you start watering a course, the wind blows it about a bit, and grass that's dormant in the sand will grow. I left Dubai for a time as the course was nearing completion and returned when it was slated to open. I was horrified by what I saw—instead of barren areas adjoining the fairway, there were corridors of six-foot-high grass. This made Arabian Ranches seem so narrow that it was incredibly intimidating. It's a great credit to the greenskeeping staff that they've managed to control the grass; it's a constant battle."

There are enough golf courses in Dubai (and a number of others in development) to justify a golf vacation in this direction. These include the two courses at Emirates Golf Club (Majlis and Wadi), the four courses at Jumeirah Golf Estates (Earth, Fire, Water, and Wind), The Montgomerie, The Dubai Creek Golf and Yacht Club, and the Four Seasons Golf Club Dubai. But the city's zest for over-the-top architecture and its incredible energy level are equal attractions. (Writing in *The New Yorker*, Ian Parker described the city as having developed so quickly, "it seems to be living in its near future, rather than its present.") "The growth that Dubai has seen is simply amazing," Ian said. "When I first went in 2000, one of my hosts took me to a symposium where presales for new residential projects were being conducted. One was called the Marina Project, which was described as having fifty high-rise buildings, twenty with fifty stories or more. Three years later, it was finished—it houses 150,000 people." Must-see creations include the distinctive Burj-al-Arab, billed the world's first "7-star" hotel, whose design mimics the billowing sails of *dhow*, the traditional Arab sailboats that ply the Gulf below; the Palm Islands, a series of manmade islands in the Persian Gulf that will one day hold luxury homes, retail establishments, and hotels, and which from the sky resemble palms; and Ski Dubai, the Middle East's first year-round, indoor ski resort and the largest snow park in the world—no small technological feat in a place where temperatures can reach 120 degrees!

IAN BAKER-FINCH, a native Australian, is best known for winning the 1991 British Open at Royal Birkdale. He has won tournaments on all four major tours and holds sixteen titles worldwide. Ian also served as Presidents Cup cocaptain with Peter Thomson in 1996, and as captain's assistant to Gary Player for the International Team in 2003, 2005, and 2007. He is also the president of Baker Finch Design, which has been developing courses including Kennedy Bay in Australia, Arabian Ranches Golf Club in Dubai, and coming courses in Ireland and St. Croix. He recently teamed with Gary Player Design to execute golf course design concepts worldwide. A well-recognized TV personality, Ian provides golf commentary for CBS Sports on the PGA Tour and for TNT at the Open Championship; he has also worked with ESPN and ABC Sports. Ian is involved in a number of charitable events and causes in both the U.S. and Australia, for which he has helped raise over a million dollars. He lives with his wife and two children in Florida.

If You Go

▶ **Getting There:** Dubai is served from the United States via many carriers, including Aeroflot (212-9442300; www.aeroflot.ru) and Emirates (www.emirates.com). The weather is most comfortable during the winter months, from November through March.

▶ **Course Information:** Par 72 Arabian Ranches plays 7,691 yards from the black tees. "I don't recommend people playing from there," Ian said. "We have the long tees, as Arabian Ranches might one day be a Dubai Open venue." Green fees range from Dhs 325 to Dhs 385—approximately $85 to $105.

▶ **Accommodations:** There are eleven guest rooms available in the clubhouse at Arabian Ranches (+971 4 366 3000; www.arabianranchesgolfdubai.com). There's a wide range of accommodations in downtown Dubai, from the world's only 7-star hotel to one- and two-star properties. Thatsdubai.com provides a list of available options.

DESTINATION

46

FOUR SEASONS CARMELO

RECOMMENDED BY **Brian Robbeloth**

Be it because of a predilection for soccer, a modest median income, or a distaste for things British, golf is not a big game on the South American continent. Golf's small place in South America's sports pantheon has resulted in a finite number of courses (roughly the same number found in Scotland). Architectural history buffs know that Alister MacKenzie passed through Argentina in 1930 and left a few fine layouts at the Jockey Club in Buenos Aires. Trivia fans may know that the world's highest course, La Paz Golf Club, lies at 10,800 feet, outside the capital city of Bolivia, and that Ushuaia Golf Club in Tierra del Fuego is the world's southernmost golf course. A small minority may have heard of Four Seasons Carmelo, considered by most to be Uruguay's—and by many, South America's—finest course.

"Take out a map of the earth and ask someone where Uruguay is, and half the people will put their finger in Africa," Brian Robbeloth said. "Say that Carmelo is just a twenty-minute prop-plane flight north of Buenos Aires, and people have a clearer idea of where we are. A majority of our guests come up from greater Buenos Aires, though not many come specifically for golf. We only have about 4,000 rounds a year. Those who do visit the course have a very relaxing experience, as there's generally no one in front of you and no one behind. You feel very much like it's your own course."

If you don't have a map of South America in front of you, Uruguay is a small nation of 3.5 million people sandwiched on the South Atlantic coast between monolithic Brazil to the north and Argentina to the south. Like Buenos Aires, which is just across the estuarial waters of the Rio de la Plata, Uruguay has a European flair; much of the population has Italian or Spanish roots. Uruguay enjoys a temperate climate year-round—atmospherically and politically; it boasts a high standard of living and offers its citizens an impressive array of social services. The town of Carmelo (population 20,000) lies at the beginning of the Rio de la Plata, which is formed by the convergence of the Uruguay and Paraná rivers. The river and its surrounding wetlands form the backdrop for Four Seasons Carmelo and its fine, if vastly underutilized, golf course. "Uruguay's tourism slogan is 'Uruguay natural,' and that applies well to Carmelo," Brian continued. "The course is surrounded by water—in fact, sixteen of the holes were created out of marsh and swamp, and water still comes into play on those holes. All that water attracts over 130 different bird species. Thanks to Carmelo's uncrowded nature, a visitor can play a hole, go to the tee, and just sit and look at the countryside. No one is going to rush you."

Carmelo was designed by Randy Thompson and Kelly Blake Moran, both of whom had worked previously with Robert von Hagge. Thompson is based out of Santiago, Chile, and does most of his design work in South America. Despite the challenges of working with swampland and a modest construction budget, the Thompson-Moran team crafted a routing that's friendly to newer players and a good test for low handicappers. "Carmelo has wide-open fairways, and the rough is cut low so players can find wayward shots," Brian described. "Water is omnipresent, but it's mostly on the sides. Oddly enough, it's usually the better players who find water, as there are more forced carries from the back tees, and more temptations to take risky lines over the marsh. The green sites are all elevated and well bunkered; everyone can lose shots around the greens."

Brian's favorite sequence of holes at Carmelo comes at the conclusion of the front nine. "The 7th is a long par 3 (210 yards from the back) with an all-water carry to a two-tiered green. The only place you can bail out is to the right of the hole, where a large bunker waits. To make things trickier, the wind is often in your face. Eight is a long (565 yards) par 5 that doglegs around a lake to the left; the lake curves around behind the green. I've only seen one player make this hole in two. If you're laying up (as most do), you have to be careful of a bunker in the middle of the landing area. A conservative play here leaves a long third shot into the green. From the tee of the par 4 9th (445 yards) the clubhouse looms ahead, with another lake on the left and bunkers guarding the left side of the fairway. The temptation is to take a direct line and try to fly the bunkers, though playing to the right is much wiser, as the wind is going to knock down all but the strongest shots.

"It's been interesting for me to watch the development of golf in Uruguay and Argentina, and how people approach the game," Brian added. "It's evolving from an old people's sport to a pastime that's embraced by younger generations. The success of Argentines Angel Cabrera and Eduardo Romero has generated great enthusiasm for the game. People enjoy the exercise; most walk and pull their own cart. A majority of players are high handicappers, yet they enjoy competition. They want to play their own ball, and they're not going to give someone a two-foot putt. They live by the rules, and will quit a game in a huff if they sense that their playing partners aren't abiding by them. Overall, the golf infrastructure is improving. There are more schools opening, and the schools' pros are getting training from Scotland's R & A. More courses are beginning to pop up, and more people are playing."

A stay at Four Seasons Carmelo affords you an opportunity to rub shoulders with some of Buenos Aires's elite, but also exposes you to the campesinos of this agricultural region. "I find that the local people are very genuine and proud of their heritage," Brian said. "There are excellent wines made from Tannat grapes, which produce a full-bodied red—many bottles cost all of four dollars U.S.! They go very well with the local beef. For nongolfers, there are pristine beaches on the river and some historical sightseeing nearby (including Colonia del Sacramento, a Portuguese settlement dating back to 1680). Overall, Carmelo has a very warm, countryside feeling.

"If you're looking for more excitement, you can get all the chaos you want in Buenos Aires [population thirteen million], just across the Rio de la Plata."

BRIAN ROBBELOTH is director of golf at Four Seasons Carmelo. A second-generation golf professional hailing from Arizona, Brian has served as director of golf at both Kino Springs Golf Club (Nogales, Arizona) and Estrella del Mar Golf and Beach Resort (Mazatlán, Mexico).

If You Go

▶ **Getting There:** Most guests will reach Carmelo via Buenos Aires, which is served by most major carriers. From Buenos Aires, it's a short flight to Carmelo; charter service can be arranged by Four Seasons Carmelo. Golf can be played year-round; peak season is the austral summer—December and January.

► **Course Information:** The Four Seasons Carmelo course (+598 542-9000; www.fourseasons.com/carmelo/golf.html) plays 7,158 yards from the back tees to a par 72; it has a slope rating of 136. Green fees are $140 USD.

► **Accommodations:** Carmelo Four Seasons (800-819-5053; www.fourseasons.com/carmelo) offers twenty bungalows and twenty-four suites.

DESTINATION

47

HO CHI MINH GOLF TRAIL

RECOMMENDED BY **Hal Phillips**

"The model for golf trail travel in the United States is fairly predictable," Hal Phillips began. "You play a course, drive a bit, stay in a Fairfield Inn, eat at a Bennigan's or Hooters, play another round of golf, and repeat the exercise each day. There's nothing about the adventure that's culturally enlightening, nor is that really the traveler's goal. The Ho Chi Minh Golf Trail is a bit different. While the courses you visit are first-class, there's nothing intrinsically exotic about the golf. It's all about the place. You take to the Ho Chi Minh Golf Trail to experience a bit of Vietnam itself."

The Ho Chi Minh Golf Trail was created to link together golf properties in the north and south of Vietnam, and to make the trip more logistically feasible for overseas travelers. "As Vietnam opens up to visitors and prospers, golf courses are being built at a steady pace," Hal explained. "When a few friends and I threw out the name 'Ho Chi Minh Golf Trail,' we kind of laughed. After a week of thinking about it, though, we thought it might just work." The Trail links together seven golf courses—three in the north, four in the south. Visitors can do the southern or northern portions of the Trail, or the whole Trail, a trip that can be customized for ten to sixteen days' duration. "People generally do a customized version that incorporates the full Trail or something close to it, as they're not going to travel to Vietnam just for the weekend," Hal added.

The trip generally begins in the north, in Hanoi. "Hanoi has a very French feeling, which is something you see throughout Vietnam, given its colonialist past," Hal continued. "It's evident in the architecture, and in the pace of life here. There's a thriving art scene in Hanoi, and we encourage guests to take in some of the galleries." Your Hanoi golf begins at Kings' Island Country Club, the north's first course, located just outside of town. The parkland layouts (there are two eighteens here) wind through forested hills and around

OPPOSITE:
The Da Lat Palace course is the high point— in terms of both altitude and layout—of the Ho Chi Minh Golf Trail.

a dominant central lake feature—indeed, the courses and clubhouse are reached by a per-manently on-call water taxi operated by the club. After a day of sightseeing that includes stops at Ho Chi Minh's Mausoleum and the Temple of Literature (Vietnam's oldest univer-sity, dating from 1076 A.D.) and meals at a few of Hanoi's trendier restaurants, you'll travel to Halong Bay and board the *Émeraude*, a replica of a colonial-era steamship. On the two-hour drive to the sea, you witness the dichotomies of twenty-first-century Vietnamese life firsthand, where farmers working the rice paddies with their water buffalo stand directly beside burgeoning industrial parks and manufacturing operations.

At Halong aboard the *Émeraude*, you cruise out among the bay's limestone karst islands, which rise spectacularly from the sea. "Sitting back in a wicker chair, sipping a martini, you feel as if you're visiting the nineteenth century," Hal described. After a night on the ship you disembark to play the Chi Linh Star Golf and Country Club, considered the north's premier tournament course (Asian PGA Tour events have been held here). Chi Linh unfolds around a lake that comes into play on a dozen holes, and ends with a monumental par 5 that stretches 660 yards, and plays uphill.

You'll next fly south to take up the Ho Chi Minh Golf Trail in its namesake city, for-merly known as Saigon. "It's an incredibly vibrant city," Hal said. "It's teeming with people, and everyone seems to be going someplace with great purpose, in the same way people rush about in Hong Kong or Manhattan." There are several days to tour Ho Chi Minh City with your own guide; visits to some of the local markets provide great insight into Vietnamese culture. "The people expect their food to be extremely fresh," Hal explained, "and you can be pretty sure that your chicken or fish is harvested the day you enjoy it. The emphasis on fresh food explains the sprawling markets."

Two of the Trail's golf highlights come on the southern leg of the journey, at Da Lat Palace Golf Club and Ocean Dunes Golf Club. Da Lat, which lies at 5,000 feet, is a short plane ride from Ho Chi Minh City. Da Lat was once a popular vacation retreat for French colonials; its rugged, pine-covered hills are an unexpected treat for many visitors who do not expect to find mountains here. Thanks to its elevation, Da Lat is also refreshingly cool, earning it the nickname "City of Eternal Spring." The layout, created by sports marketing giant IMG, stretches 7,009 yards through rolling hills and along Xuan Huong Lake. "When you're playing the course, you see the Sofitel Da Lat Palace Hotel across the lake," Hal recalled. "It's an old hunting lodge restored to its 1920s glory. Guests stay at the Sofitel while visiting Da Lat, and you simply must have dinner there the evening after golf. The

DESTINATION

48

dining room is incredibly opulent, like something out of an Edith Wharton novel. The last time I was there, I couldn't help but think that golfers visiting Scotland could not possibly enjoy such a scene, except maybe at Gleneagles. It's that posh, that Old World."

From the mountains of Da Lat you'll descend to the coastal fishing and resort town of Phan Thiet to play Ocean Dunes. With its wide fairways, imposing sand dunes, and ocean views, this Nick Faldo design is the closest approximation of a links course that you'll find in Vietnam . . . though you won't mistake it for Turnberry. "There's a small Buddhist temple located entirely within the routing at Ocean Dunes, just off the third green," Hal recalled. "There's another much larger temple right off the 10th fairway. I was playing once and there was a wedding going on. The air was redolent of incense, and there was the white noise of chanting in the background. It's one thing to hear church bells on the course, but this was bizarre and exhilarating. You're very aware that you're playing a game that's not native to the culture."

HAL PHILLIPS spent seven years reporting for and editing daily newspapers before joining *Golf Course News* as editor in chief in 1992. During his tenure he would oversee the launch of both *Golf Course News Asia-Pacific* and *GCN International*. In 1997, Hal left to form his own media consulting firm, Phillips Golf Media, which soon morphed into a fully fledged media, marketing, and IT agency, Mandarin Media—though he never stopped writing. His published pieces have since appeared in *Golf* magazine, *Sports Illustrated*, *Travel & Leisure Golf*, *Portland Press-Herald*, *LINKS*, and *Golfweek*.

If You Go

▶ **Getting There:** The Ho Chi Minh Golf Trail generally can begin in either Hanoi or Ho Chi Minh City (Saigon). Both cities are served by many major carriers, including Cathay Pacific (800-233-2742; www.cathaypacific.com).

▶ **Course Information:** The seven courses on the Trail are all regulation, championship-quality courses. For more details, visit www.hochiminhgolftrail.com.

▶ **Accommodations:** All of your accommodations and many of your meals are included as part of your Ho Chi Minh Golf Trail odyssey. You'll stay in some of Vietnam's finest hotels, including the Sofitel Da Lat Palace.

A WELSH SAMPLER

RECOMMENDED BY **John Hopkins**

As far as golf travel to Great Britain is concerned, Wales—the small nation of three million souls tucked between the central section of England and the Irish Sea—is simply not on the radar for most Americans. John Hopkins, the golf correspondent for *The Times* (of London) and a Welsh native, has a more practical explanation. "Wales doesn't have the pure number of courses (approximately 200) that Ireland and Scotland have, nor do we have the marquee courses. Just as important, we don't have the tourist spend that those countries have. What most outsiders don't realize is that we have more castles (641), a history of music and drama, a distinctive culture with warm and friendly people, and tremendous scenery (including 687 miles of coastline)—and a dozen truly great courses. Since Wales is a small nation, you can take in the highlights of each region (North Wales, Mid-Wales, Southwest, Southeast) in a relatively short time without spending all of your trip driving. For all these reasons, Wales is the undiscovered golf secret of Europe."

With the Ryder Cup coming to the Celtic Manor in Newport, South Wales, in October of 2010, the secret may soon be out. For the interim, John shared a few of his favorite venues, sweeping from the north to the south, and beginning at Nefyn and District Golf Club, on the Llyn Peninsula. Nefyn may be the world's only twenty-six-hole track—the first ten holes are shared by the Old and the New; the Old's last eight holes head out onto a precariously narrow peninsula called The Point (playing golf here has been likened to playing on an aircraft carrier). The New's final eight unfold along an inlet. All are fine holes, but The Point is particularly alluring, with the sea on one side, sandy beaches on the other, and, on a clear summer evening, a vista of the Wicklow mountains, fifty-seven miles across the Irish Sea. Both James Braid and J.H. Taylor contributed to the course's initial incarnation. "I started visiting Nefyn when I was a boy," John continued. "We'd go on holiday from England, and I played there for ten or eleven successive summers. The inland holes [The New] were built because some of the members found The Point too narrow and potentially dangerous, and because there were paths leading down to the beaches and there were conflicts with nongolfers. The 13th hole (a 405-yard par 4) is still vivid in my memory. You tee off from the top of a cliff. If the wind isn't against you, you can try to carry the inlet that's on your left to give yourself a short-iron to the green, though it requires a brave drive. A more cowardly tee shot plays to the right, where you have a long-iron in. It's so much more satisfying to go over the inlet."

From Morfa Nefyn, you'll head down the coast to Mid-Wales and the sleepy resort town of Aberdovey and its beloved links. James Braid had his hand in the design of the course here, as did Harry Colt and Herbert Fowler. The efforts of this brain trust were not wasted, as this romp through the dunes near the mouth of the Dovey River showcases a wealth of original and creative holes. "I learned about Aberdovey from the great *Times* golf columnist Bernard Darwin," John explained. "His love of the course helped foster my affection. The links are sandwiched between the hills and railroad line on one side and the waters of Cardigan Bay on the other. Visitors can still take the train from London to Aberdovey; you step off the train and walk a hundred yards and you're at the club. Its proximity to the railway helped bring the course to some prominence. Aberdovey has a half-dozen tremendous holes, but the 17th—a 428-yard par 4—is my favorite. It runs between the railway line on the left and the rest of the course on the right. You have a lot of room to the right, and the wind coming off the water will blow the ball back toward the fairway. It's the second shot that's tricky, as it's difficult to judge how the wind will impact your shot."

The last stop on your introductory tour of Welsh golf gems brings you to the southeast and Royal Porthcawl, perhaps the one venue that's widely known beyond Wales' borders. This classic links, with nary a tree on the field of play, lies on the Bristol Channel and Swansea Bay. The water is in view from every hole, thanks to the sloping land and the absence of large dunes; without a break from the sea, the wind is always in play. The club itself was established in 1891 and the first eighteen-hole layout appeared in 1899. It was refined twice in the coming decades, first by Harry Colt (1913) and then by Tom Simpson (1933). "Royal Porthcawl could easily host major professional events if there were space to accommodate the crowds," John said. "It's that good. The two bars in the clubhouse look just as they did in the 1890s, when it was moved to its current resting spot by the sea."

The tone for a round at Porthcawl is set immediately with three strong par 4s right along the beachfront. For John, a peak is reached at the diminutive par 3 7th, a mere 122 yards. "It shows that a one-shotter doesn't have to be 190 yards into the wind to be difficult. It's so beautifully bunkered that you can be on the green in places and almost need to chip the ball. I compare it to the 7th at Pebble Beach and the 8th at Royal Troon, in terms of challenge."

JOHN HOPKINS is the golf correspondent for *The Times* (of London), a position he has held since 1993, following in the footsteps of Bernard Darwin. He has covered golf for *The Sunday Times* (where Henry Longhurst was a predecessor) and for *The Times* for the past thirty years. John has attended more than 120 of the four annual major championships, sixteen Ryder Cups, twelve Walker Cups, and ten Solheim and Curtis Cups. Born in Wales, John now lives in the Vale of Glamorgan, although much of his time is spent traveling the world attending golf events. He is the author of *Golf Wales* (www.golfwale-suk.com), a guide to Welsh courses.

If You Go

▶ **Getting There:** If you decide to begin your exploration of Wales in the north, fly into Manchester or Birmingham, England, and drive west from there to Nefyn. If you begin in the south, fly into London's Heathrow Airport or Cardiff and head west to Porthcawl.

▶ **Course Information:** Nefyn Golf Club (+44 1758 720102; www.nefyn-golf-club.com) in the village of Morfa Nefyn plays 6,609 yards from the back tees to a par 71. Green fees range from £21 to £44. Aberdovey Golf Club (+44 165 476-7493; www.aberdoveygolf.co.uk) in the village of Aberdovey plays 6,870 yards to a par 72. Green fees range from £35 to £45. Royal Porthcawl (+44 165 678-2251; www.royalporthcawl.com) in the town of Porthcawl also plays 6,870 yards to a par 72. Green fees range from £75 to £120.

▶ **Accommodations:** The Official Visit Wales golf website (+44 870 121-1251; www.golf-asitshouldbe.com) lists package options and a variety of accommodations.

CHAMBERS BAY GOLF COURSE

RECOMMENDED BY **Bruce Charlton**

Many who peered over the edge of a quarry abutting the Burlington Northern Santa Fe Railroad line and Puget Sound west of Tacoma saw a hopeless eyesore—piles of sand and rock, the ravages of a hundred years of gravel mining.

Bruce Charlton, president and chief design officer of Robert Trent Jones, Jr. Golf Course Architects, and his associates saw a U.S. Open venue.

"When I first saw the RFP [Request for Proposal]—before I even visited the site—it jumped off my desk," Bruce recalled. "Ninety percent of the golf courses in the Pacific Northwest were getting their materials from the quarry—you figure it's got to be pretty good stuff. And the long-term plan the county had put together was very ambitious. The golf course would be part of a larger public works project and serve as a filter for runoff to Puget Sound. When I actually visited the site, it blew my mind. First I was taken by the scale of the place. The bottom of the quarry was 200 feet down. Not only was Puget Sound right there, but there are islands and boat traffic. You have views of the snow-capped Olympic Mountains across the sound—at least on a clear day. And perhaps most important of all, the county had held onto the quarry's mining permit. Give golf architects a chance to be in the sand and move it around as they see fit, and you've given them a golden opportunity. It meant we could take portions of the site down fifty feet or raise other portions one hundred feet. As the saying goes, we were happy as kids in a sandbox, the biggest sandbox we'd ever played in. We had a great canvas to work with, a climate where we could use links grasses, and the freedom to move sand any way we wanted—it was a win-win-win."

From your arrival at Chambers Bay, it's evident you're in for a very different experi-ence. There's a modest clubhouse as you pull into the parking lot, but no course—until

219

you walk into the clubhouse or to the edge of the precipice and look down. The field of play lies in the cavity, some 240 acres resting 200 vertical feet below, in the void created by the former mining operation. Massive mounds, unruly waste areas "the size of some northeastern states" (to quote golf writer Jeff Wallach), and brilliant hues of green delight the eye. Barges and occasional sport fishing boats ply the bay. On the south edge of the course, there are several Stonehengesque structures—sorting bins from the quarry days. After you pay your green fees, a minibus transports you down the hill to the practice range and the first tee. Your opening drive—to a fairway shared with the 18th hole on the left and bordered by massive dunes on the right—confirms your initial suspicion that a special morning or afternoon lies ahead.

OPPOSITE: Puget Sound is in view from every hole at Chambers Bay; here it frames the 12th green (foreground) and the 15th (below the lone fir tree).

With its Pacific Northwest seaside locale, its Ballybunionesque dunes and hummocks, its mercurial winds, and its exhilarating elevated tee shots, Chambers Bay cannot help but court comparison to the courses at Bandon Dunes. There are certainly parallels in the experiences. But one great difference that underlines Bruce and company's accomplishment is that much of the links land that you see at Bandon was there before the courses were plopped down, and everything at Chambers was manufactured. "John Ladenburg [the Pierce County executive who spearheaded the partnership that brought the course into being] was out on the course with Ryan Moore, an up-and-comer on the PGA Tour who grew up nearby. After the first three or four holes, Ryan said 'It's really cool the way you wound the course through these dunes.' John laughed and said, 'Everything you've played so far has been created.' That's one of the best compliments we've received."

There are many standout holes at Chambers Bay, and Bruce Charlton classified some of his favorites by various criteria. "For pure aesthetic beauty, I like the 9th, the 14th, and the 15th. The 9th (a par 3 that plays 227 yards from the back) is the highest hole on the course, and the ball drops nearly 100 feet from the back tee. You have a panoramic view of everything from here. The par 4 14th is a long (530 yards!) cape hole that also starts high up and plays sharply downhill over a huge waste area we call the 'pit of despair.' Fifteen is a little downhill par 3 that plays down to the bay over waste bunkers and is framed by the lone tree on the course, a modest fir. [Could it be Chambers' answer to Pebble Beach's lone cypress?] From a working-with-the-land perspective, I love the par 4 6th—we found the green site pretty much as it exists now. There are dugouts on the right side that reminded us of church pews; they come into play if you try to cut off too much of the dogleg. I also like number 7, as it plays against the eastern slope of the quarry,

DESTINATION

50

showing how high the land was before the pit. (Seven is a monstrous par 4 that plays 508 yards uphill, with the Gobi desert guarding the right side the whole length of the hole, two prominent mounds standing in the middle of the fairway somewhere between most players' second and third shots, and a boldly contoured green with a prominent false front.)

"If you were to put a gun to my head, I'd say that the 16th (a 425-yard par 4) is my favorite. It plays right next to Puget Sound, right along the railroad tracks, like so many of the old courses in Scotland. It has a little Pebble Beach–style green. One of the things that are special to me about this hole is that we lowered a thirty-five-foot bluff that had been created by the mining along the entire length of this hole, so the holes adjacent would feel more like they're on the water.

"Something that's a little different at Chambers Bay is that the teeing grounds aren't all flat. We wanted to make them an extension of the fairway, and give some side-slopes, some cross-slopes; this would give more skilled players spots to place the ball to manufacture certain kinds of shots according to the conditions on the given day. This was not an easy concept to explain to the shapers!"

As many readers may know, the U.S. Open prophecy of Bruce Charlton, Jay Blasi, Bobby Jones, John Ladenburg, and others involved with Chambers Bay from the beginning has come to pass: the course will host the 2010 U.S. Amateur Open and the 2015 U.S. Open. Bruce recalled a walk of the property with USGA officials before Chambers opened. "We hadn't finished the grassing, but as we walked the layout, one of the USGA folks turned to Bobby, Jay, and myself and said 'Have you considered talking to the Royal and Ancient to see if they'd like to have the British Open here?'"

BRUCE CHARLTON is president and chief design officer of Robert Trent Jones, Jr. Golf Course Architects, which he joined in 1981 after graduating from the University of Arizona with a degree in landscape architecture. Bruce's more than fifty international designs include Trans Strait Golf Club and Yalong Bay Golf Club in China, The Marshes Golf Club in Canada, Skjoldenaesholm Golf Center in Denmark, Bjaavann Golfklubb and Holtsmark Golf Club in Norway, and Sky Hill Jeju Country Club in South Korea. His U.S. courses include Arizona National Golf Club; The Bridges at Rancho Santa Fe and Rancho San Marcos Golf Course in California; Raven Golf Club at Sandestin, Florida; Osprey Meadows at Tamarack Resort, Idaho; Prairie Landing Golf Club and ThunderHawk

Golf Club in Illinois; Southern Highlands Golf Club in Nevada; Chambers Bay in Washington; and University Ridge Golf Course in Wisconsin. Bruce is a member of the executive committee of the American Society of Golf Course Architects and has served as the organization's president. He lives in Los Altos, California, with his wife, Maridee, and their daughter, Casey.

If You Go

▶ **Getting There:** Chambers Bay is in the Tacoma suburb of University Place, roughly thirty miles south of the SeaTac Airport, which is served by most major carriers.

▶ **Course Information:** Chambers plays 7,585 yards from the championship teal tees, to a par 72; it has a slope rating of 135. Green fees range from $69 to $155, depending on when you visit. Chambers Bay is a walking-only facility.

▶ **Accommodations:** The Tacoma Regional Convention and Visitors Bureau (800-272-2662; www.traveltacoma.com) lists lodging options around Pierce County.

Published in 2009 by Stewart, Tabori & Chang
An imprint of Harry N. Abrams, Inc.

Text copyright © 2009 Chris Santella

Photograph credits: Pages 2, 72, 76, 98, 122, 142, and 170: © Evan Schiller/golfshots.com; pages 12 and 146:
© Mark Hill; page 14: Photo courtesy of Pannónia Golf & Country-Club; pages 16, 44, 86, 96, 126, 138, 150,
160, 192, and 220: © John and Jeannine Henebry; page 22: © Dick Durrance; page 28: © Gary Lisbon; pages
32 and 156: © Mike Bell; page 36: © Rob Brown; pages 40, 56, 68, 102, 114, 174, 178, and 200: © Brian Morgan
Golf Photography; page 52: © Robin Moyer/robinmoyer.com; page 64: © Sperone Golf Club; page 82:
Photo courtesy of Golfclub Am Mondsee; page 90: © Greg Norman Golf Course Design; page 130:
Photo courtesy of Boyne Resorts; page 134: © Fairmont Hotels and Resorts; page 164: Photo courtesy
of Oitavos Dunes; photograph by Brian Morgan; page 182: © Aidan Bradley Photography; page 188:
© Grant Leversha; page 200: photo courtesy of Arabian Ranches; page 212: © Peter Steinhauer

Library of Congress Cataloging-in-Publication Data
Santella, Chris.
Fifty more places to play golf before you die : golf experts share the
world's greatest destinations / Chris Santella ;
foreword by Jeff Wallach.
p. cm.
ISBN 978-1-58479-793-7
1. Golf courses—Directories. 2. Golf resorts—Directories.
I. Title. II. Title: 50 more places to play golf before you die.
III. Title: Golf experts share the world's greatest destinations.
GV975.S194 2009
796.352—dc22
2009000579

Editor: Jennifer Levesque
Designer: Anna Christian
Production Manager: Tina Cameron
Fifty Places series design by Paul G. Wagner

This book was composed in Interstate, Scala, and Village typefaces

Printed and bound in China
10 9 8 7 6 5 4 3 2 1

harry n. abrams, inc.
a subsidiary of La Martinière Groupe

115 West 18th Street New York, NY 10011
www.hnabooks.com